DER GEIST Volur

MW01594862

Editor: Trevor Blake
Co-Editor and Designer: Kevin I. Slaughter
Copy Editor: Anonymous

First Printing: October 2018
[Stirner, Max] Blake, Trevor; Kevin I. Slaughter
ISBN 978-1-944651-11-4
ISSN 2639-5339
Philosophy
Reference

SUBSCRIPTIONS are not available at press time.

BULK RATES and DISTRIBUTORS and INSTITUTIONS please inquire.

UNIONOFEGOISTS.COM

UoE West Coast

Der Geist, Inquiries & Reviews

LETTERS:

Trevor Blake
P. O. Box 2321
Portland, OR 97208-2321
UNITED STATES

PACKAGES:

Trevor Blake
715 NW Hoyt Street #2321
Portland, OR 97208-2321
UNITED STATES

UoE East Coast

UnionOfEgoists.com, *Stand Alone*

LETTERS & PACKAGES:

Union of Egoists
444 Maryland Ave #7940
Essex, MD 21221
UNITED STATES

EMAIL:

editor@unionofegoists.com

Not responsible for unsolicited materials.

INTRODUCTION

Der Geist documents the philosophy of egoism as published between 1845 and 1945. Egoism begins in 1845 with the publication of *Der Einzige und sein Eigentum* (*The Ego and His Own*) by Max Stirner. While egoism does not end in 1945, this century-mark serves as a practical delineator for our work.

Der Geist places special emphasis on certain authors and groups from this time period. We refer to these authors (see back cover) as our "Union of Egoists" after this passage from *Der Einzige*:

> We two, the State and I, are enemies. I, the egoist, have not at heart the welfare of this 'human society,' I sacrifice nothing to it, I only utilize it; but to be able to utilize it completely I transform it rather into my property and my creature; i. e., I annihilate it, and form in its place the Union of Egoists.

Der Geist is descriptive, not prescriptive, regarding egoism. *Der Geist* aids the study of egoism but it is not itself in advocacy of egoism. The reader may find what is published here true or false, beautiful or ugly, strong or weak, left or right, praise-worthy or damnable, but it will always be accurate to the source. Whether the reader studies our work to build it up or tear it down, our scholarship is above reproach. Our only instance of advocacy is that the reader make haste to buy multiple copies of all our publications.

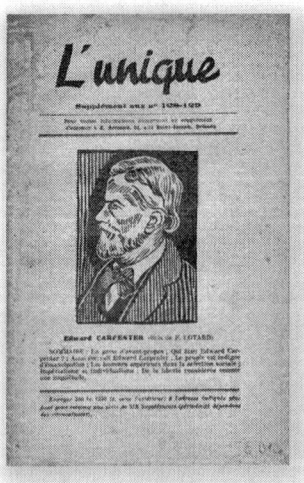
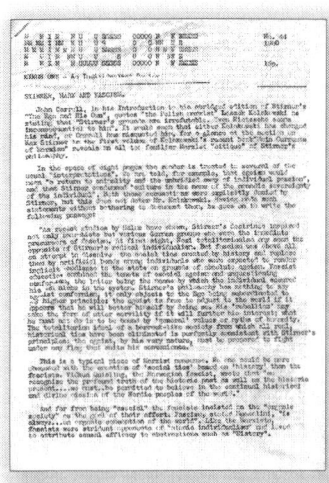

Der Geist puts the imp in the imprimatur of English-language egoist publishing. Follow along as we show an unbroken chain between Stirner and *Der Geist*. Max Stirner published *Der Einzige und sein Eigentum* in 1845. This was the year Émile Armand discovered anarchism via the magazine *Les Temps nouveaux*. The French translation of *Der Einzige* was published as *L'unique et sa propriété* in 1899. Three years later Armand became expressly an individualist anarchist and not a communist anarchist. Armand published a series of journals advocating individualism, the last of which was *L'Unique* (the Unique) between 1945 and 1953. S. E. Parker read *The Ego and His Own* in 1961. In 1962 published *Anarchism and Individualism / Three Essays* by Émile Armand. In a 1993 interview, Parker said Armand personally charged him to reanimate the individualist anarchist movement in all the countries of the English language.' Parker published a series of journals advocating individualism, including *Ego* in 1982. In 1992 Parker gave Svein Olav Nyberg permission to reprint essays from *Ego* in Nyberg's journal *Non Serviam*. *Non Serviam* transitioned from print to internet at i-studies in 2011. Kevin I. Slaughter and Trevor Blake founded UnionOfEgoists.com and *Der Geist* in 2016. With the assistance of Nyberg, the content of i-studies was folded into UnionOfEgoists.com in 2016. With the authorization of his granddaughter, the archive and publishing responsibilities of S. E. Parker were granted to Kevin I. Slaughter in 2018. From Stirner, to Armand, to Parker, to Nyberg, to *Der Geist*. We need no blessing for our endeavors, but our pedigree is pleasant indeed.

Since the first issue of *Der Geist* the editors have published schol-

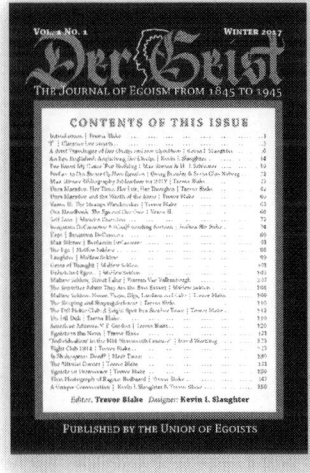

arly egoist material each month. This includes high-quality facsimiles with new introductions of historic work as well as original research. Significant expenditures have been made to acquire unique books on the Unique philosophy: these books in turn inform our research, freely published at UnionOfEgoists.com. The works of S. E. Parker are being published by Kevin I. Slaughter in cooperation with the Parker estate at SidParker.com.

The Muslim *jihad* against *Der Geist* reported in our founding issue continues. It's the same old slanders, the tired old threats, and yet we report with confidence their intimidation and calumny has had no effect. Not one of Allah's faithful has produced as much work as we, or as worthy. Rapacious they are, runts riddled with resentment. Some few of Allah's faithful have sympathy for what we are doing but cry out that we are doing it *wrong*. They say they too are in favor of the individual, but only individuals *like them*. There's just no pleasing them. Write what they don't like, you are *haram*. Write what they like, it's a false front. Remove what was written, it's a cover-up. Publishing of anything is agreement with everything published and the birth-to-death life of the author, they say (note they seem to be able to publish without a similar stain of sin). Their own literature is evil when it is we who praise it. Well, they are welcome to their rejection of the self, for all the good it does them. If it were not for this brief mention, what reason would anyone have to know they ever existed?

This issue of *Der Geist* includes egoist essays that have not seen print for nearly a century, and some that appear here for the first time. The editors hope that our delight in original research into the history of egoism is complementary to your own interests and studies. You can show your support by purchasing our books. You can show your disgust and disagreement by purchasing copies of our books and destroying them. Something for everyone!

—TREVOR BLAKE,
editor, *Der Geist*
KEVIN I. SLAUGHTER,
editor, UnionOfEgoists.com

BENJAMIN DeCASSERES

Benjamin DeCasseres (1873-1945) was a writer in many forms, from editorial to poetry, and the author of many books and booklets. Born in Philadelphia, PA, he dropped out of school and got a job as an office boy for the Editor-in-Chief of *Philadelphia Press* newspaper. At age 16, he was promoted to proofreader and occasionally wrote editorials and reviews.

In 1899, at age 26, he moved to New York and got a job with the *New York Sun* as a proofreader. His first freelance article was published in 1902 and shortly thereafter he began contributing to Elbert Hubbard's various magazines, often ghostwriting.

In 1906 he moved to Mexico to work for the English-language edition of *El Diario*, but that only lasted a year before he moved back to New York and worked and lived there for the rest of his life. He passed away in 1945.

> "We have had in the last two thousand years Christian-baiters, Jew-baiters, free-speech baiters, free-thought baiters, and now in this country we are afflicted with the Pan-baiters. They chase the great god from the eating places, from literature, from the 'movies,' from the stage, from the painted canvas, from the great poem, from the hearts of the human... Pan-baiting is the veritable business of our lawmakers and sectarian pundits. If they ever discover that sunlight intoxicates they will attempt to gouge the eyes out of the God of Day himself." —Benjamin DeCasseres, "The Pan-Baiters," from *The Judge*, April 3rd, 1920.

Benjamin DeCasseres in 1932 admiring a portrait of Benedict de Spinoza
at a party celebrating this 300th birthday. Care of Union of Egoists.

ARTICLES IN THIS SECTION

Two works from *The Detroit Jewish Chronicle* concerning Benjamin DeCasseres and Nietzsche. "Germans, Jews and France" was published November 15, 1935 (page 6); "I Dance with Nietzsche" was published December 11, 1936 (page 13).

"Hate Everlasting" first appeared in *The Philistine* Volume 27 Number 4 (September 1908).

The first of two essays from *The Double Dealer*, this from vol. 1, no. 1, 1921. This is the first of three installemnts of a series called *Tales of a Psychometric Reporter*. Subsequent interviews were conducted with Diogenes and Cleopatra.

The Double Dealer is called a "Little Magazine" in the same vein as Dora Marsden's *The Freewoman* (and subsequent name changes), Margaret Anderson's *The Little Review* and Elbert Hubbard's *The Philistine*.

DeCasseres in *The Detroit Jewish Chronicle*

UNCREDITED (1936)

Germans, Jews and France /
DeCasseres Shows Nietzsche Hated the German People

Benjamin DeCasseres, eminent writer and critic, descendant of the family of Baruch Spinoza, is the author of a pamphlet, *Germans, Jews and France*, in which is compiled a series of statements from the writings of Nietzsche. This pamphlet, published by the Rose Printers & Publishers, Inc., 91 Runyon St., Newark, N.J., proves that contrary to the claims of Nazis, Nietzsche hated the Germans and had the highest respect for the Jews. DeCasseres took the excerpts in this pamphlet from the 15 volumes of Nietzsche's works. In a foreword to the booklet he states: "In Germany his universal doctrine of Will-to-Power and his ideal of Superman have been used by professors and mob-masters as philosophy to excuse their atrocities, their sadism and their totalitarian-state crimes. But they have carefully concealed what you will find in this booklet."

In his attack on the Germans, Nietzsche is quoted among other things as follows:

'German intellect' is my foul air.
When I try to think of the kind of man who is opposed to me in all my instincts, my mental image takes the form of a German.
Even the presence of a German retards my digestion.
I can no longer abide the (German) race.
I was condemned to the society of the Germans.

Under the caption "Germany and the Germans," Mr. DeCasseres has compiled a chapter of quotations among which we read:

The Germans have not the faintest idea how vulgar they are.
The spirit of Germany — soft, swampy, slippery soil.
A man lowers himself by frequenting the society of Germans.

Another chapter in which he condemns the Germans is titled

"German Culture." Three of the 31 pages are devoted to a discussion of the Jews, and he says of them:

> What a blessing a Jew is among Germans!
> This race (the Jews) should not be irritated without necessity. Therefore anti-Semites should be expelled from Germany.
> Since Wagner's return to Germany he has condescended to everything that I despise — even to anti-Semitism.
> In respect to cleaner intellectual habits, Europe is not a little indebted to the Jews; above all, the Germans as being a lamentably *deraissonable* race, who, even at the present day, must always have their 'heads washed.' It has always been the Jews' problem to bring a people to *raison*.
> It was Heinrich Heine who gave me the most perfected Idea of what a lyrical poet could be.
> Among Jews I did, indeed, find taste and delicacy toward me, but not among Germans.
> The Jews are beyond all doubt the strongest, the toughest and purest race at present living in Europe.

A two-page chapter on France pays tribute to the French as compared to the Germans he despised. Nietzsche is quoted as saying: "We Germans are nearer to barbarism than the French."

I Dance with Nietzsche / DeCasseres "Dances with Nietzsche"

Benjamin DeCasseres, lineal descendent of Spinoza, ranks among the outstanding authorities on the German philosopher, Nietzsche, whose name has been invoked by Nazis in the campaign against the Jews. A short time ago DeCasseres published a pamphlet entitled "Germans, Jews and France by Nietzsche" in which he compiled the writings of this German to prove that instead of being a hater of Jews, Nietzsche, rather, favored them and despised the Germans.

A great lover of Nietzsche, DeCasseres is continually writing commentaries on his works and one of the most interesting of his pamphlets entitled "I Dance with Nietzsche" has just come off the press. It is procurable at 50 cents from him, care of the Blackstone Publishers, 118 W. 27th St., New York City.

Benjamin DeCasseres

The title of this pamphlet is derived from Nietzsche's having been referred to as the Dancing Philosopher. A most interesting tribute to Nietzsche is contained in this pamphlet in which DeCasseres writes:

> No one has stimulated me over a longer period of time than Nietzsche. Merely to pick up one of his books after reading him for 30 years gives me a great thrill, physical, mental and metaphysical. With a book of his in my hand I feel precisely like a person who holds a bomb.
>
> I love him because he inflames every part of my psysic and physical life. He is perpetual ecstasy, orgasm. He inflames me to intellectual anger, quite often, as well as to dancing with intellectual joy. But I thank him for infuriating me almost as much as I thank him for penetrating me with mental ecstasy. For whether I agree or disagree with him, he causes my emotions, my thoughts, my nerves to dance.

Elsewhere in this booklet, Mr. DeCasseres states:

> The prophet and writer in Nietzsche are straight out of the Old Testament. He is of the strain of Isaiah and Jeremiah, King David and Jesus. He is an Old Testament Jew transposed to a modern sensibility. He is par excellence the Puritan. He is in no sense Greek. He is Oriental. His 'funeral of God' is somewhat pathetic, for he has resurrected Jehovah under the name of the Superman. 'Sacrifices' are demanded in the name of the Superman. Here is the God of the Old Testament again.

DeCasseres calls Nietzsche "the greatest psychologist of all time, one of the greatest poets who have ever lived, one of the master-stylists of world-literature, one of the Six Colossi of Thought, the incarnation of all militant Individualists that have been and the protagonist of those to come — sublimely beautiful soul whose like we shall probably not see again."

HATE EVERLASTING
BENJAMIN DECASSERES   (1908)

Philosophic and poetical gentility have prated for thousands of years of the creative and the transforming power of love. I wish to say something of the creative and transfiguring power of hate, of the eternity of hate, the morality of hate, the rejuvenating power of hate, the cosmic, social and artistic necessity of hate, the splendour and sublimity of a sublime aversion.

Repulsion, hatred, opposition — "Room for me or thou diest" — are the conditions of individuality. Universal love would insure universal catalepsy. Passion creates, not love. The spark is struck at the moment of impact. All movement is conditioned in hate. All so-called progress — which is merely motion lapsing from goal to goal — is the revolt of the Present against the Past. Eternal insurrection, challenge, hatred and battle are the conditions of the survival of anything. Hate, dissatisfaction, discontent, contempt, are the sacred fires that must be forever kept burning. What man dislikes shall be his God; what man hates shall be his golden Cain-brand; the mystical blasphemers, the upsetters, the deniers, the sappers, those who seek to lay in hate the rotten rookeries of cosmic and earthly complacency in the dust — it is they who are the Holy Ghosts of Time, the great Space-patrol, our moral guardians, the night-watch of those who love and sleep. Prometheus gnawed by a majestic hate, still parleys with Jove, and Lucifer, now as forever, still hurls his imprecations from his earth-hell and pits his mystic steeds of black against the milk-white geldings of the Lord of Incense.

In nature, hate and murder are conditions of survival.

All beauty is the mask of hate. Forms, elements and worlds flush space, appealing to the contemplative aesthetic sense merely as craven images of beauty; but to the clairvoyant intellect they are the painted records of an everlasting strife, mere glitter from the gutters of Time, the gonfalons of triumph raised above the Cosmic shambles, the jubilees of hate triumphant.

This opposition, hatred, strife and demoniacal impulse to arise into being and maintain a foothold there at any cost, is a commonplace of existence, but not a commonplace in human apprehension. To live is to prey and to prey is to hate. The Hindu says all life is guilt.

All feasts celebrate the death of something; they are the gambols of the peoples on corpses; the high wassail of hate, the gratulations of survival.

The Persian invocation says, "Give me this day an enemy." An enemy helps me to create, drives me to my wits' ends, distends my ego and puts a thousand thousand eyes in my brain. An enemy's eye cast on me in hate has fructifying power; self rushes to the center of gravity, instinct and intellect arise armed cap-a-pie, from within the penetralia of the soul there issues the primitive being aureoled in his acrid aversions.

Hate is ethical. Hate destroys trammels. It is the moral passion that burns up codes, parchments and jousts with the oleaginous optimism that pins paper roses in the hair of the Lord of Things as they are. Byron and Nietzsche and Ibsen rowelled the dugs of the Arch-Stupidity that litters us, and the Worlds we expire on like a field-woman accouches her burden. "Moral Indignation," which is the name moralists give to hate, is a barometer of mental and spiritual life. Each is known by his aversions, by the things he seeks to destroy. They who hate life are greater than life; they who love life are stillborn; they are ravished only by sex and kitchen scents.

The life of the individual is like the life of a beast of prey.

The totality of each man's movements from the cradle to the grave if they could be put into a design, into a kind of composite photograph, would resemble the circular, attentive movement of an animal about its prey.

There is the thing the Will seeks to pounce on and make its own, and we circle around it for years sometimes, drawing closer and closer, crushing with the paws of egotism all that gets into our way.

All great literature is rooted somewhere in an ideal hatred, in a recognition of the eternal *qui vive* of man; the perception that man is greater in his overcomings than in his resignations.

The revealer must be a good hater. He moves the world because the lever of intellectual perspective rests on the fulcrum of aversion. The *Prometheus* of Æschylus, the *Timon* of Shakespeare, the *Zarathustra* of Nietzsche, the *Ghosts* of Ibsen — *The Philistine Magazine* — are the fruits of a sublime rage, a perfect frenzy of contempt, hatred and militant spite.

Tales of a Psychometric Reporter: How I Interviewed Bacchus
Benjamin DeCasseres   (1921)

"The chief wants to see you."

It was the office boy of my Sunday editor who spoke. I had a standing start, but I beat him back to the desk by three feet. The chief glared at me, hid his income tax blank in a drawer, and said mildly:

"Benson, go get an interview with Bacchus on prohibition."

My ears stiffened like a man's in the heart of the Sahara who has just been told there was a brewery on the other side of the next sandheap.

"You mean, boss, Bacchus, the original rum-hound?" I falsettoed, my voice seeming to come out of my eyes.

"Why, you don't think I mean the president of the Fudge Union, do you?" he said, hiding his patent space cutter in a drawer. He swiveled around to his Give-Them-the-Gate list. I knew the interview was over. I knew I had to get that interview with Bacchus or sign up somewhere else. I ambled up Broadway.

"What! You never heard of psychometry?"

I turned quickly. Two men, arguing excitedly, disappeared in the crowd. But the word "psychometry" remained. Was it a hunch?

What in the name of the Sacred Soup of Siam was psychometry? I turned into the nearest branch public library and feverishly turned the leaves of the dictionary. Psychometry is the big trick among the Occult Squad. It is "divination by touch." If you have psychometric powers you can call up the history of a man or an object by holding it in your hand. Hold your sweetheart's fan and all her flirtations will swim into your brain. Press a dollar of your landlord's in your hand and his profiteering crimes will be yours.

A great thought-flash illuminated me. Maybe I had that power— maybe I was a born psychometrist.

Another tremendous thought opened its barrage on me. If I had that power, why couldn't I by holding a bottle of old Burgundy in my fist and letting my cerebrum and cerebellum float on their backs in my consciousness evoke Bacchus and interview him?

But the bottle of Burgundy? It was as rare as tobacco in a ten-cent pack of Mahomet cigarettes, worth its weight in radium, and the lamps of the Eighteenth Amendment sleuths were full upon me.

One thought pumps another out of the old pipes of our memory.

I knew the butler in the mansion of "Old Pale Ale" Smith, the millionaire clubman up the Avenue. He and his family were at Palm Beach. Would the butler let me in old "Pale Ale's" wine cellar, estimated to contain about a billion dollars' worth of joy-juice?

Easiest thing ever. Tom Pourboire not only let me in the cellar, but spread a table for me down there, and yanked out a bottle of old Burgundy. I was his bonus-fide guest, under the law; he should worry and so forth.

I buried my fist in the dust of the bottle of the unopened wine—I wasn't after the drink this time—and called: "Oh, Bacchus, God of Booze, be with me now! You've done me many a rotten turn before the Ginmillennium set in—now you can do me a good turn. Appear, dear old Bac.!"

There was a terrible commotion away back in the dark of the vast cellar. Boxes and casks rumbled and fell. Into the light walked Bacchus. He was flesh and blood!

I knew he was Bacchus instinctively, although he had a Jack Dempsey haircut, wore a bartender's white apron, a sport shirt, and a Japanese silk crepe tie.

His face was the image of the late Johnny Walker. In his hand he carried a large bottle of wine with the Latin inscription in huge letters burned in the glass:

"From the cellars of Nero, Chateau Orgy, Anno 61."

He took a seat on a cask of whiskey after shaking hands with me and addressing me as "Benson old pal."

"Talk low and quick," he said. "I've got old John Barleycorn, Grandfather Gambrinus and Little Lord Absinthe back in that corner. We're hiding from the raiders. Ain't this a great disguise? I dress according to the country I'm in. We're trying to drink up everything Old Pale Ale has in his cellar before he gets back from the beach.

"The gang back there are sick—it's a big job drinking all the stored stuff. You know I could always carry it. Where there's a wine there's a way with me.

"Well, go ahead, Benson, and spill your wheeze."

"What are you doing on earth, anyway, Bac., old boy?" I asked, looking at my questionnaire in my hat.

"Well, you humans put it over on us when the Great War got going. Mars took over all the gods and put Olympus on a war basis. He said as this was the biggest job he'd ever pulled off, he wanted clear heads about him, and that all the gods had to cut out late hours and all drink. Of course he was looking straight at me.

"John Barleycorn he said he could handle, because John could never handle himself. He didn't care much about Gambrinus, said he was only a German milkman after all. He didn't even argue with Little Lord Absinthe—just booted him into the Styx, where old Charon kept kicking him along in disgust. But for me he had some respect; said I was as ancient as the earth, the gods and everything else. Tapping me on the bean wouldn't do any good, so he granted me a vacation to the Earth till he got through with his job.

"I took the three of them back there with me, and I've certainly had my troubles ever since. Truth to tell, Benson, we've been so lit up since we landed that I don't know how I'll get that gang back. Pegasus has become an old spavin. We're stuck."

"How did prohibition in America hit you?" I went on in a business-like voice, giving him the second question in my hat. Before Bacchus could answer a voice that sounded like a singing coal mine came over the top from the abysmal darkness of the cellar:

"Hoorah! Hoorah! I'm a guy in wrong.

"The Constitush has got me an' me bar-lee-corn!"

"Can it!" shouted Bacchus. "No wonder they've got you wandering from cellar to cellar."

"That's the guy that put me on the blink. Why, his breath blew out the fires of Vulcan one morning Up There," continued Bacchus, addressing me.

"John was a low-brow, never could disguise himself and was always singing out of turn. It's the bad actors that kill all the fun, and that fellow has certainly been a bad actor, although when there's any sickness around there ain't a better friend than—"

"But about prohibition, Bac?" I insisted, my reportorial instinct on the alert.

"Let me tell you, Benson," said Bacchus, poking his bottle of Nero's finest under my nose to emphasize his opinions, "That prohibition serves you right. You disgraced a god—that's me. I invented the finest toothache and grouch killer ever known—me and Gambrinus; but you Americans chucked us and picked up with that rowdy John Barleycorn and his crazy pals. You took that roughneck to your own tables, introduced him to your families, and when he couldn't come to you, you invented a Family Entrance and went to him, ramming me into hideous red-ink joints and keeping me alive on bum table d'hotes.

"It is written of old—by some wise guy or other—that no one can offend a god and get away with the goods. Why, I'm the oldest of the gods, the best and the healthiest. You made me a Cinderella and lavished all your love on that demon back there. Look at me now.

"Look at this rig I've got to dress in! Look how I've got to go sneaking around from cellar to cellar with that rowdy back there—and I a god, celebrated by poets and prophets in all ages, the friend of all real human beings, the father of laughter, the inventor of merriment. You've busted my heart— that's what you have!"

And dear old Bacchus began to blubber all over the cask. Near me a voice began to croak.

"I'm old! I'm old! I'm beer that's near. I'll go to Jersey to get up cheer!"

"That's old Gam." said Bacchus, drying his eyes. "He too's in bad with me."

"Will you come back, Bacchus?" I asked, that being the third question pasted in my hat.

"Did you ever hear of anything that didn't come back?" answered Bacchus, righting himself into something of his old-time form.

"As badly as you've treated me in this country, I'm going to stick. As a matter of fact, since Mars still has all his war measures in force up there, I've got to stick. I need America as much as you are going to need me. I am about twenty-thousand years old and I've traveled a bit, as your classical sharps will tell you.

"Well, Benson, I can tell you that there never was a nation or a people who tried to can me who didn't start toward Davy Jones' locker, which is, as you know, quite different from a club locker.

"There never was one exception. The Eskimos never had any use for me— and look at them! Ice eaters and the North Pole for a bathtub, and never a drink of the old stuff to warm them up. Jack Frost has got their souls as well as their bodies, and it'll get yours if you don't look out. Where life flourishes there am I; where it begins to frost, I retire."

"What will be the ultimate effect of prohibition, Bac.?" I asked.

"Long faces, the dark brown taste of a universal mental grouch, and the disappearance of pleasure. Seriousness, my boy, has destroyed more people than even old John, back there."

"Are you and the crowd back there going to get away with all this stock?" I asked.

"Every bit of it without drawing a cork. When Old Pale Ale gets back his bottles will be as he left them, but there'll not be a drop in them."

"How's that done?"

"We absorb it by psychometric thirst." Bacchus replied with a tremendous guffaw. His laugh was so loud that it startled me, and I took my hand off the bottle of Burgundy.

Bacchus had disappeared.

Benjamin DeCasseres

THE FATAL SMILE
BENJAMIN DeCASSERES   *(1922)*

There is nothing more astonishing than the smile that is born in hell; astonishing, final and fatal. Hamlet had it in fiction. Heine had it in life.

This smile—mute in Hamlet, fantastic in Heine—is the hilarity of grief. Pain intensified finally mocks itself. A sigh frozen in the blood of the brain will sparkle like a diamond.

Those who live always in the sun know the nameless things she breeds. The corruption of light generates that unhallowed smile. The thumbscrews and racks of knowledge are the presses that squeeze the hemlock into the cup of perception.

The luminous sorrows of Heine evaporated in an eternal tra-la-la. Hamlet, feigned seriousness in order to strangle the laugh that would have rent his brain. Jules Laforgue, the French poet and fantastic, put an ice poultice over his heart and died of a cold. His smile gored the heart out of all his illusions.

It is the crack in the urn of thought—this brain-chuckle. It is a strange hieroglyphic from a hidden wisdom. It is an eccentric fata morgana that plays above the graves in the heart. It is the gibbet of remorse and the succubus of conscience.

The sick have the Fatal Smile when the doctor tells them they must die before the night is out. Nature has it in the deep of the woods late of a sunny afternoon in the mid of October. It lit up the brain of Iago when looking at the corpses of Othello and Desdemona. It gnawed at the brain of Balzac till it crumbled. Between Swift and the world that fatal smile hovered like an asbestos curtain.

Disembodied the Fatal Smile is the Spirit of Circumstance, the immutable gray eye of Fatality. It was the fire-fly with the wintry flame that circled the head of Orestes and Oedipus, Napoleon and Edgar Allan Poe. It is the invisible satyr in worlds and destinies, the star vainly licked by the flame of a myriad hells.

Passionless, smiling Sphinx! Alembic of all sorrows! Mecca of all the fabled antinomies of science and reason! Star in the forehead of Lucifer! Cold Bethlehemic light hovering over the manger of geniuses destined to strange Gethsemanes and pensive Calvaries!

The slow evaporation of ideals and their condensation into nebulous comic visions; the slow massacre of brazen hopes; the murderous concussion of Will and Reality—it is these causes that bring about that sadic vengeful smile—that guffaw in hell.

The Ideal is a vague clarion-call sounding from impossible summits. The fatal smile forever muffles it. It is the eyeball of the dark; a blending of the sibilant maledictions of ironic well-wishers.

The whole universe becomes a microscopic silhouette against the background of that infective tra-la-la. It is sometimes born of the slings and arrows of outrageous pleasures as in the case of Francois Villon. With Nietzsche the smile hung like a black sun over the ravines of light in that dionysiac soul.

Over all that Jules Laforgue wrote there lies that smile like a glistening spider-web. Schopenhauer and Leopardi live forever in a mansion in those ironic skies.

The paladins of pleasure and the patriarchs of sin take that Fatal Smile for final concubine. The oval face of Grief is at last touched to ice by that transfiguring chrism. The legioned visions of impenitent minds cannot go beyond that fatal sign. The passion of those monstrous brains that seek to trick God out of his omniscience are blasted by the light on that tragi-comic Horeb!

Bayreuth
Rathaus mit Brautgasse, links Geburtshaus Max Stirner

2

MAX STIRNER / *THE EGO AND HIS OWN*

Max Stirner (October 25, 1806 – June 26, 1856) was a German philosopher. He is often seen as one of the forerunners of nihilism, existentialism, postmodernism, and anarchism, especially of individualist anarchism. Stirner's main work is *The Ego and His Own* (*Der Einzige und sein Eigentum*). This book is the wellspring of egoism. *Der Einzige* was first published in 1845 in Leipzig, and has since appeared in numerous editions and translations.

> "I write because I wish to make for ideas, which are my ideas, a place in the world. If I could foresee that these ideas must take from you peace of mind and repose, if in these ideas that I sow I should see the germs of bloody wars and even the cause of the ruins of many generations, I would nevertheless continue to spread them. It is neither for the love of you nor even for the love of truth that I express what I think. No — I sing! I sing because I am a singer. If I use you in this way, it is because I have need of your ears!" —Max Stirner, *The Ego and His Own,* translated by Steven T. Byington.

Postcard featuring Max Stirner's birthplace
by Kunstverlagsanstalt Bruno Hansmann, Cassel. (no date)

ARTICLES IN THIS SECTION

The Worker and the Government Max Stirner
For over a century, Steven T. Byington's 1907 English translation of *Einzige* was the only complete translation of Stirner's opus. Aside from Byington, all translations were partial. This non-Byington translation is uncredited, and appeared in the *Anarchist Soviet Bulletin,* edited by Marcus Graham, for December 1919.

What is Good? What is Evil? Dr. James L. Walker
An excerpt from *Liberty and the Great Libertarians / an Anthology on Liberty, a Hand-book of Freedom* by Charles T. Sprading (Los Angeles: Charles T. Sprading 1913). The book includes Edmund Burke, Thomas Paine, Thomas Jefferson, William Godwin, Wilhelm von Humboldt, John Stuart Mill, Ralph Waldo Emerson, William Lloyd Garrison, Wendell Phillips, Josiah Warren, Max Stirner, Henry D. Thoreau, Herbert Spencer, Lysander Spooner, Henry George, Benjamin Tucker, Pierre Kropotkin, Abraham Lincoln, Auberon Herbert, G. Bernard Shaw, Oscar Wilde, Maria Montessori and others.

Good Reading to Sharpen Mental Teeth Uncredited
Uncredited review first published in *NOW / A Journal of Affirmation* Volume VI Number 7 (March 1906). An early review of the first book published on egoism in North America.

My Thought's on N'ought! William Flygare
Der Geist offers the first publication of Flygare's translation of Goethe's poem "Vanitas!" The title of the preamble to *Der Einzige* is *Ich hab' Mein' Sach' auf Nichts gestellt,* the first line of Goethe's poem. There are few English-language translations of this preamble. H. J. Schirmer, in his 1897 translation, presents it as "I've Based My Cause 'Pon Nothing." In the 1907 Byington translation we read it as "All Things Are Nothing to Me." In John Carroll's "Roots of the Right" edition on 1961 we read it as "I Have Founded My Affair on Nothing," and in the Land-streicher translation it is Englished as "I Have Based My Affair on Nothing." According to S. E. Parker in *non serviam* number 18 (Spring 1999), Swedish-Japanese Buddhist scholar William Flygare translated the original poem in full for an edition of *The Ego and His Own* planned but never published by The Libertarian Book Club. William Flygare's (1916-1997) published works include two collections of poetry: *Presence* in 1972 and *This* in 1993 (revised 1995); the monograph *Montaigne-Shakespeare* in 1978. He contributed reviews, translations and poetry to Parker's egoist journals *Minus One* (1963) and *Ego* (1982).

Max Stirner Bibliography Addendum Trevor Blake

L'Unique et sa propriété Max Ernst

The Unique Individual Uncredited
An uncredited review of *The Ego and His Own* first appeared in *The New Age* New Series Volume 1 Number 16 (August 15th, 1907). *The New Age* was edited by A. R. Orage. Orage was a reader of Oscar Levy and employed Anthony M. Ludovici as an art critic. As sympathetic as *The New Age* was to egoism, Dora Marsden (true to form) gave *The New Age* a steady working over in her magazines.

I've Based My Affairs on Nothing Malcolm Green
This unique English translation of the preamble to Stirner's *Einzige* was made by Malcolm Green for the book *Black Letters Unleashed / 300 Years of Enthused Writing in German* (London: Atlas Press, 1989). We thank Mr. Green for permission to reprint from this highly recommended work.

The Worker and the Government

Max Stirner
Uncredited Translation   (1919)

Governments do not let me come to my value, and continue to exist only through my valuelessness: they are forever intent on getting benefits from me, that is exploiting me, turning me to account, using me up, even the use they get from me consists only in my supplying a proletariat; they want me to be "their creature."

Pauperism can only be removed when I as ego realize value from myself, when I give my own self value. I must rise in revolt to rise in the world.

What I produce, flour, linen, or iron and coal, which I toilsomely win from the earth, etc., is my work that I want to realize value from. But then I may long complain that I am not paid for my work according to its value: the payer will not listen to me, and the governments likewise will maintain an apathetic attitude so long as it does not think that they must "appease" me that I may not break out with my dreaded might. But this "appeasing" will be all, and, if it comes in to my head to ask for more, the Governments turn against me with all force of their lion-paws and eagle-claws: for they are king and beast, they are lion and eagle. If I refuse to be content with the price that they fix for my ware and labor, if I rather aspire to determine the price of my ware myself, that is "to pay myself" in the first place I come into conflict with the buyers of the ware. If this were stilled by mutual understanding the Governments would not readily make objections; for how individuals get along with each other troubles them little, so long as therein they do not get in their way. Their damage and danger begins only when they do not agree, but, in the absence of a settlement, take each other by the hair. The Governments can not endure that man stand in a direct relation to man; it must step between as mediator, must intervene. What Christ was, what the saints, the church were, the Governments have become — to wit, "mediator." It tears man from man to put itself between them as a "spirit.". The workers who ask for higher pay are treated as criminals as soon as they want to compel it. What are they to do? Without compulsion they don't get it, and in compulsion the Governments see a self-help, a determination of price by the ego, a genuine, free realization from its property, which they can not admit of. What then are the workers to do? Look to themselves and ask nothing about the Governments.

But as is the situation with regards to my material work, so it is with my intellectual too. The governments allow me to realize value from all my thoughts and to find customers for them (I do not realize value from them, that is, in the very fact that they bring me honor from listeners, and the like); but only so long as my thoughts are their thoughts. If, on the other hand, I harbour thoughts that they do not approve (make its own), then they do not allow me at all to realize value from them, to bring them into exchange, into commerce. My thoughts are free only if they are granted to me by the Government's grace, if they are by the Government's grace, then they are the Government's thoughts. They let me philosophize freely only so far as I prove myself "philosopher of the Governments"; against the Government I must not philosophise, gladly as they tolerate my helping them out of their "deficiencies," "furthering" them. Therefore as I may have only an ego most graciously permitted by Governments, provided with their testimonial of legitimacy and police pass, so too it is not granted to me to realize value from what is mine, unless this proves to be theirs, which they entrusted me with. My ways must be their ways, else they restrain me; my thoughts their thoughts, else they stop my mouth.

The Governments have nothing to be more afraid of than the value of me, and in nothing must they be more carefully guarded against than on every occasion that offers itself to me for realizing value from myself. I am the deadly enemy of the Government's, which always hovers between the alternatives, they or I.

What is Good? What is Evil?
Dr. James L. Walker (1913)

What is good? What is evil? These words express only appreciations. A good fighter is a "good man" or a "bad man" — both words expressing the same idea of ability, but from different points of view. To the beggar a generous giver is a good man. To the master a servant is good when he cheerfully slaves for the master. A good subject is one obedient to his prince. A good citizen is one who gives no trouble to the State, but contributes to its revenues and stability. Evil is only what we do not find to our good, but what we have to combat. A horse is not good because strong and swift if he be "vicious"; that is, if we find him hard to tame. A breed of dogs is good if readily susceptible of training to hunt all day or watch all night for the benefit of the owner. A wife is "good" if she will not be good to any man but her husband.

The love of money within reason is conspicuously an Egoistic manifestation, but when the passion gets the man, when money becomes his ideal, his god, we must class him as an Altruist. There is the characteristic of "devotion to another," no matter that that other is neither a person nor the social welfare, nothing but the fascinating golden calf or a row of figures. We Egoists draw the line of distinction between the Egoist and the devotee. It is the same logically when a person becomes bewitched with another of the opposite sex so as to lose judgment and self-control, though this species of fascination is usually curable by experience, while the miser's insanity cannot be reached. The love-sick man or woman has the illusion dispelled by contact with the particular person that caused it; but in certain cases absence or death prevents the remedy from being applied, and in some of these instances the mental malady is lifelong.

Good Reading to Sharpen Mental Teeth
Uncredited (1906)

Philosophy of Egoism, by James L. Walker. Published by Katherine
   Walker, Denver, Colo. For sale by Benj. R. Tucker, Box 1312 N.
   Y. City, and by H. P. Replogle, Box 1307, Denver, Colo. Price, 75c
   and 35c, according to binding.

This book is a labor of love on the part of the publishers. It may be
classed as a treatise upon Philosophic Anarchy, though the author
rather denies this and calls it "Individualism." The author was a
deep and logical thinker. Any one accepting his premises will be carried along to his conclusions. It is good reading for one to sharpen
his mental teeth upon, because it is full of philosophical reasoning.
Personally I am not able to decide upon its value, for it is the an-
tithesis of my "Soul Culture" philosophy. That the author is a man
well posted and one who fortifies his positions by sound reasoning
is evident on every page. The place and use of such reasoning the
world must decide.

My Thought's on N'ought!

William Flygare

(2000)

My thoughts 'n' oughts are nothing fixed
    Hooray!
for Joy's the world that's downed unmixed
    this way!
and all who'd be good mates of mine
to clink 'n' drink just suit me fine
for lees of life and wine!

I'd trained my trade on gold 'n' gain
    Hooray!
but so I sold my joy for pain;
    I say,
the coins were rolling here and there,
but every time I chased a where
the here was over there.

To women then I gave my heart
    O belles!
but how those damsels made me smart
    O hells!
The false were true to others, true,
but true ones bored me through and through;
the best ... were not for woo.

Next, I thought I ought to roam
    Hooray!
but then I lost my ways of home,
    that way,
and nothing seemed to suit me quite,
the board was bad, the bed a fright,
and no one got me right.

I tuned my dream to name and fame
    Excel!
but better men put me to shame

O hell!
or when I gave some good I had
they made me out to be a cad;
my good was worse than bad.

I sought the right in battle might
    Hooray!
and often was our might so right
    (hooray!)
the enemy's land was ours to run;
but still the score was won to none,
and a leg became undone.

So now I call my calling nought
    So what!
The world's all mine that comes unsought
    that's what!
Now that it's song and sup all day,
come clink 'n' drink me all the way
these lees to the last hooray!

Max Stirner Bibliography Addendum
Trevor Blake
(2018)

Max Stirner Bibliography (OVO: Portland 2016) by Trevor Blake is the most complete bibliography of Max Stirner ever published in English. Happily, more commentary on Stirner has emerged and will likely emerge for decades to come. *Der Geist* will publish addenda to *Max Stirner Bibliography* until these additions are gathered in a future edition.

"The Origin of Nihilism" from the *Edinburgh Evening News* (May 17th, 1879) page 3. A similar article appears in the *Dublin Daily Express* (May 19th, 1879) page 5. See also "A Brief Travelogue of *Der Einzige und Sein Eigenthum*" by Kevin I. Slaughter in *Der Geist* Volume 1 Number 1 (October 2017).

The writer says that the first Nihilist societies were formed by Russian students about the year 1859, and the doctrines they adopted were chiefly derived from a book which did not generally have any Nihilist tendencies, Buchner's *Force and Matter*. The circulation of this work in Russia was forbidden by the Government; and the consequence was that it was secretly introduced into the country, and a lithographed translation of it was passed from hand to hand. It was read with avidity by the Russian youth, together with another German work, by Max Stirner, called *Property and the Individual*, which had also fallen under the ban of the Russian censors. Out of these two books, the former of which preached materialism and the latter Socialism, the Russians evolved the doctrine of Nihilism, which they also professed to find in popular works, notably Buckle's *History of Civilization*.

∉

"Reviews / The Philosophy of Anarchism" from the *Pall Mall Gazette* (February 29th, 1896) page 4.

Mr. Zenker is an enlightened observer of the various currents of thought by which vast groups of mankind are swayed hither or thither, and not seldom to irreconcilable extremes. From his calm standpoint he tries fairly to describe what he sees. He traces the history of Anarchism back to some sects in the Middle Ages and down to our time, dealing more specially with Proudhon, Max Stirner, Bakunin, the school of Kropotkiin, and Élisée Reclus.

∉

"United Foreign Circles: English Section" from the *Bradford Daily Telegraph* (November 20th, 1901) page 5.

A paper was read before this Section on Tuesday evening by Mr. G. H. Evans, "Anarchism and its Theories." The lecturer treated his subject in a very able manner. He commenced giving an account of the growth of Anarchist views from the 12th Century down to the present time. also gave a descriptive account of the lives and works of Proudhon, Max Stirner, Bakunin, and Kropotkin.

∉

Lucifer, the Light-Bearer Third Series Volume 7 Number 43 Whole No 994 (November 5th, 1903) page 1.

As the proletarian has nothing to lose, his "nothing" is not in need of government protection. On the contrary, he can only gain when state protection is taken away from the favored. — Max Stirner

∉

Stirner / Grundlagen zum Verständnis des Werkes "der einzige und sein Eigentum" by Hermann Schultheiss (Ratibor: Gedruckt bei F. Lindner 1906).

Inaugural-Dissertation zur Erlangung der Doktorwurde, der philosophischen Fakultat der Koniglichen Universitat Greifwald vorgelegt und mit deren Genehmigung zum Druck beforderf vom Herman Schultheiss. Sein wiffenschafliche Behandlung der Gedanten Stirners wird sich nich lediglich an das historische Interesse wenden, sonderen viellicht noch lebhafter das sustematische in Unspruch nemen.

∉

"Max Stirner's Anarchist Gospel" in *Current Literature* Volume XLII Number 5 (May 1907) pages 535-538.

Sixty years ago, a book entitled *Der Einzige und sein Eigentum* (generally translated *The Individual and his Property*) was published in Berlin. It has been described as "the most revolutionary book ever written," and its author, Max Stirner, was perhaps the leading intellectual precursor of modern philosophical anarchism. When he died, in 1856, in comparative poverty and obscurity, his theories had made but little headway; but during the years that have passed since then both book and author have commanded increasing study and respect. It begins to look as if Max Stirner might yet take rank with the great philosophic thinkers of the Nineteenth Century. He exerted profound influence over Nietzsche, and, in the opinion of no less an authority than Eduard von Hartmann, his work surpasses that of Nietzsche "by a thousand cubits." *Der Einzige* has been translated into French, Spanish, Russian and Italian; and critical studies popularizing its arguments have appeared in almost all the European countries. George Brandes, a critic of rare discernment, is one of Stirner's interpreters, and John Henry Mackay, the German poet, has written his biography. On Mackay's initiative a suitable stone has been placed above Stirner's grave in Berlin, and a memorial tablet upon the house in which he died; and this spring another tablet is to be set upon the house in Bayreuth where he was born in 1806.

An English translation of *Der Einzige*, which has just appeared in New York under the title, *The Ego and His Own*, makes Stirner's gospel accessible for the first time to American and English-speaking readers. He is difficult to read, and his oddities of composition and terminology tend to obscure his meaning. "There is nothing more disconcerting," one of his French commentators has confessed, "than the first approach to this strange work. Stirner does not condescend to inform us as to the architecture of his edifice, or furnish us the slightest guiding thread... The apparent divisions of the book are few and misleading. The repetitions are innumerable. At first one seems to be confronted with a collection of essays strung together, with a throng of aphorisms... But, if you read this book several times; if, after having penetrated the intimacy of each of its parts, you then traverse it as a whole — gradually the fragments weld themselves together, and Stirner's thought is revealed in all its unity, force, and depth."

∉

"The Philosophy of Anarchism" in *The Public* Volume X Number 486 (July 27th, 1907) page 403-405.

Max Stirner, whose true name is said to have been Kasper Schmidt, was an impoverished school teacher in Germany, who died fifty years ago. He had published at Leipsic [sic] in 1845 his *Der Einzige und Eigentum*, of which the book before us is the first English translation. For more than twenty years the publisher, Mr. Tucker, has contemplated an English edition, but not until now have his intentions been realized.

∉

"Conduct and Morality" by Francis Sedlak in *The Theosophical Review* Volume XL Number 240 (August 1907) page 496.

Once a Salvation Army man asked me whether I was saved. When I replied in the affirmative, he wished to know how and when my "salvation" came to me. And so I told him that some nine years ago, after youth spent in ambitious dreams, I found myself on the verge of the deepest despair. At first I wished to become a great general, then a great statesman, then a great linguist, then a great mathematician, then a great explorer of dark continents; then I began to climb down and would have been willing to become a simple civil servant, then only a humble reporter; and when I was willing to become anything at all, there seemed to be no room for me anywhere. I could not finish my studies and I had no particular proficiency in anything; at the time I was proud as Lucifer. And that's my destiny it seems to end in – suicide.

But just then the friend lent me Max Stirner's *Der Einzige und sein Eigenthum* (*The Individual and His Property*). The book expounds the most crass materialism, and in a way which caused me to shudder, although by that time I thought myself completely rid of all belief in the supernatural. The argument in the preface appealed to me immediately: a child *must* obey the father; he, as a citizen, *must* obey his superiors; these *must* obey the king; and the king is said to obey God. But who *must* God obey? No one, and therefore he is the biggest egoist; but if ultimately all is done for the satisfaction of an egoist, is not being oneself that egoist? It was then that I seemed to realize that my wretchedness was due to my continued allegiance to the conventional God; but to frame thought meant to be saved. "In short," I concluded, "I was saved when I ceased to believe in your god. In any case, such a sense of glorious freedom seized me that I was quite ready to go on living as a homeless and penniless tramp."

∉

"Max Stirner: Reincarnated Spook" by Robert Rives La Monte in *International Socialist Review* Volume VIII Number 5 (November 1907) pages 280-283.

"It is the unexpected that always happens" proves true once again. Writing some six months ago I spoke of Max Stirner's *Der Einzige und sein Eigentum* as a book which has been forgotten amid the growing consciousness of the organic solidarity of society. But soon afterward the irrepressible and talented philosophical Anarchist, Mr. Benjamin R. Tucker, published a brand new English translation of this forgotten work under the title of *The Ego and his Own*. The translation has been made with the utmost industry and sympathy by Mr. Stevens T. Byington [sic], and mechanically the book is an excellent specimen of modern book-making.

¢

"A Review of the Important Books of the Year" from *The Independent*
    Volume LXIII Number 3077 (November 21st, 1907) page 1,237.
The Ego and His Own. By Max Stirner. Tucker, $1.00.

¢

"Book Notes" from the *Dundee Courier* (February 10th, 1908) page 7.
A book which will soon published by Mr. Fifield is Mr. Steven Byr-
rington's [sic] translation of Dr Paul Eltzbacher's *The Anarchists*. It
is made up of ten studies of the foremost exponents of philosophic
Anarchism, among them Tolstoy, Nietzsche, Kropotkin, Max Stirner,
and Benjamin R. Tucker.

¢

"Literary Gossip" from the *Belfast News-Letter* (May 31st, 1909) page
    6. A similar article appears in the *Aberdeen Press and Journal*
    (May 31st, 1909) page 7.
Mr. Werner Laurie is publishing a new book James Huneker, the author of *Iconoclast*. It will be called *Egoists / A Book of Supermen*. This
work, the first by Mr. Huneker in three years, is wholly devoted to
those modern poets and masters whose writings embody the individualistic idea as opposed to altruistic Socialist sentiments. Stend-
hal, Maurice Barrès, Anatole France, Max Stirner, a forerunner of Nietzsche; the mystic Ernest Hello, J. K. Huysmans, and William Blake,
these and many others are analysed.

¢

*Liberty and the Great Libertarians / an Anthology on Liberty, a Hand-
    Book of Freedom* by Charles T. Sprading (Los Angeles 1913).
Max Stirner, pseud, of Johann Kaspar Schmidt, 1806 — 1856, individualist philosopher, writer, apostle of Egoism. Born at Bayreuth in
Bavaria. Studied philosophy and theology at Berlin and at Erlangen;
traveled; taught in young ladies' seminary in Berlin, 1839-44. His remarkable book, *The Ego and His Own* (*Der Einzige und sein Eigentum*),
translated by Steven T. Byington and published by Benj. R. Tucker,
but now out of print, was known only to a few academicians until
its recent revival through the investigations of his biographer, John
Henry Mackay, the German poet, and through the sudden fame of
the writings of Friedrich Nietzsche, who shows an intellectual kin-
ship to Stirner. A great lover of freedom, both for himself and others,
Stirner in his writings lays the philosophical foundation for political

liberty and encourages the practical development of egoism to the dissolution of the State and the union of free men.

∉

"Wisdom of the Wise" from the *Milngavie and Bearsden Herald* (January 2nd, 1931) page 6.

"One is free in proportion as one is strong." Max Stirner.

∉

Individualismo, Estética y Humanitarismo by Eugen Relgis (Madrid: Cuadernos de Cultura 1933).

Es necesario, sin embargo, bosquejar el retrato del prototipo del individualista anarquista. Un nombre y una obra se nos aparecen inmediatamente: Max Stirner, *El Unico y su propiedad*. Numerosos críticos sociales se preocupan hoy aún de este libro, que es, desde el principio al fin, un grito de libertad y de rebeldía del «yo.» Benjamín DeCasseres se ocupa de él con mucho discernimiento. A sus ojos, *El Unico y su propiedad*, expresión suprema del egoísmo y de la rebeldía, no es, sin embargo, uno de los libros más peligrosos, pues su filosofía es impracticable. Las enseñanzas de Ibsen, de Emerson, de Whitman y de Nietzsche son más «peligrosas» que el libro de Stirner. *El Unico y su propiedad* es, empero, una obra que incita al hombre a un examen de conciencia, una obra que aniquila los «santos fantasmas.» El «Unico humano» es para Stirner una especie de divinidad. Para servirla tenemos que dejarlo todo: Estado, hogar, familia, religión, todo lo que mata al alma humana. Mas, libres de esos «parásitos,» de esos «fantasmas terrestres,» no sabemos hacia qué dirigir nuestras aspiraciones. «La propiedad del Unico» parecía tener, según Kipling, el sentido siguiente: «Toma todo lo que te sea necesario para el perfeccionamiento de tu personalidad.»

∉

The following quote appears in the *Hartlepool Northern Daily Mail* (July 5th, 1939) page 2; the *Linlithgowshire Gazette* (July 14th, 1939) page 6; the *West London Observer* page 8; the *Scunthorpe Evening Telegrap*h (August 10th, 1939) page 1; the *Birmingham Mail* (August 24th, 1939) page 5; the *Wells Journal* (August 25th, 1939).

"The men of future generations," Max Stirner wrote, "will yet win many a liberty of which we do not even feel the want."

L'UNIQUE ET SA PROPRIÉTÉ
MAX ERNST
(1925)

L'Unique et sa propriété by Max Ernst, 1925.
Frottage and pencil on paper. 26 by 19.8cm

THE UNIQUE INDIVIDUAL
UNCREDITED (1907)

The Ego and His Own. Max Stirner. Trans. by S T. Byington. (A. C.
    Fifeld. 6s. 6d. net.)

In the absence of a complete English translation of the work of Nietzsche (for which, by the way, somebody or other deserves to be shot), we may be grateful for this translation of Nietzsche's John the Baptist. Max Stirner wrote sixty years ago his *Der Einzige und sein Eigentum*, in which he certainly anticipated the main ideas of Nietzsche and the most modern revolutionary school. That Nietzsche may have owed a good deal to Stirner we can certainly believe; but not for a moment can we tolerate the suggestion that Nietzsche owed everything to his forerunner. All such comparisons and valuations are utterly worthless, and make it appear that a doctrine should only be true if no more than a single person should hit on it. That two or three or a dozen people should say the same thing because it happens to be true seldom strikes the writer of introductions as even probable.

Stirner wrote his book during the seething revolutionary period of 1848, when both in Germany and in France a good deal of frothy talk was being raised on subjects such as Liberty and the Rights of Man. In some ways, such words and phrases are characteristic of most revolutionary movements. After all, if you have not cannon, what else is there to do but talk? Stirner grew more and more indignant as he recognised not only that the phrases and words meant little, but that in the mouths of most of the young Germans they meant nothing at all. He, therefore, began the enormously difficult task of endeavouring to hammer into the minds of his contemporaries the differences, and sometimes the radical antagonisms between words and realities. In this he was simply following Epictetus, with whom in other respects he seems to have had much in common. A liberal education, Epictetus said, gives a man no more than the faculty of discriminating words.

It happens, of course, that reformers today are very much like the reformers of 1848, and the reformers of Epictetus' days. In other words, Stirner's message is quite as necessary now as it ever has been since the dangerous discovery of speech. At this moment we are all employing words without meaning, and talking of things that have no real existence. Our vocabulary plays such tricks with our intellects as cause the realistic angels to weep. Stirner was mainly concerned with the two words, Liberty and Man. In essence they may be said to constitute the Alpha and Omega of liberalism in the broadest and narrowest senses. Both words are, strictly speaking, meaningless; or, at least, their meaning is so vague that their use in genuine discussion is extremely perilous. Regarding Man, for example, it is plain on a moment's reflection that we know of no such entity. One man we know, another man we know; but where is this "ghost," this "spook" (to use Stirner's words) who is not this man or that man, but Man? Yet we proceed in all our reformatory schemes on the assumption that somewhere or other there exists, or ought to exist. Man who is not any particular man, but a Being from whom all particularities have vanished by sublimation. In place of the two concepts of myriads of individuals as they are, and of myriads of individuals as they actually might be, we abstract from both, and make Man as he is, and Man as we think he ought to be. The result is that all our legislation is made to apply itself to two impossible and non-existent entities, to Man with a capital M, and to Humanity as it ought to be in a perfect state, etc. But this sacrifice of real individuals to the non-existent and impossible Perfect Man is exactly similar to sacrifices made to any other abstract Mumbo-Jumbo. The more atheistic, in fact, revolutionaries pride themselves on being, the more firmly have they made the secret substitution of a wholly imaginary ideal Man or Humanity for God.

Against this ingrained habit of men to sacrifice themselves to dragon-like ideals, Stirner inveighs with splendid zeal. He is a rare realist, and an iconoclast of the first order. He will have nothing to do with abstractions, even when they simulate the concrete form of generalisations. His single claim is that he is unique and incomparable. I am not, he says, Man, but a man. I ought not to become essential Man or to fade away into a colourless abstraction. On the contrary, my sole business is to become more and more myself. Legislation that assumes that I am like anybody else in all the world is misfit legislation; when it assumes that I am like everybody else it is simply ludicrous. No, my claim is to a special treatment of a special being; and your ideals of perfection and all the rest leave me cold because they are not my ideals.

This principle of uniqueness is really incompatible with a good deal of the modern talk of reform. The mere dangling of new communal ideals before masses of people is from Stirner' s standpoint the dangling of new halters over our necks. If it comes to a choice it might even be easier to serve a theological than a humanitarian ideal. The service of the older gods at any rate, did not require individual deification; but the service of the new god, Humanity, apparently demands the humanisation of man. Stirner again points out that a man can no more become Man than man can become God; he can only become himself. A man, however, may very well try to become what he is not; and these efforts of his are the most lamentable and tragic feature of his history. Dissatisfied with himself as he is when once he has descended to the level of comparison, he seeks to add to himself all the belauded or envied qualities of other men. That such fruit cannot possibly grow upon his tree is his secret misery; yet he endeavours to simulate their appearance. And this pathetic abandonment by a man of his own task of bringing forth his own fruit in favour of the task which other men are only too willing to put upon him, of bringing forth their fruit, is responsible for all the moral misery and deformity of the world. Deceit, lying, evil conscience are the accompaniments of' this shirking of his own destiny for him; and the submission to punishment at the hands of others for his good. All punishment being, theoretically at least, intended for the good of man, theoretically assumes both a man's consent, and a man's desire to become Man. To refuse to bow the knee to Man is the reformer's conception of blasphemy. But Stirner has some equally strong things to say of Liberty. Ibsen once remarked of Norway that it was a land of political liberty peopled by slaves. The same remark may be made of all the western European countries. Political liberties arc doubtless worth fighting for, since the light for liberty alone is liberty. But it is probable that there are more genuinely free men to the square mile in Russia at this moment than in any other country in Europe. The curse of politics is that we confound political liberty with freedom. Freedom is the will to be responsible for oneself; political liberty is permission to choose one's masters. Except for the change of régime is there any difference between serving a majority of one's fellow citizens and serving a feudal baron? Unless it can be shown (as we hold it can) that the change of mastership is for the better, there would be nothing to say for democracy. On the other hand, unless democracy is regarded merely as a means, its modified tyranny is no less a tyranny than any other despotism. Stirner, as we have said, pours the vials of his wrath upon all these vague phrases and words. His one object is to become himself; the same object he supposes is at the root of every other individual. All institutions are to be valued according as they enable the greatest number of individuals to become more individual. The more similarity the more despotism. The greater variety of individuality the greater the freedom. Political liberties, democracy and Socialism for the sake of the individual and his uniqueness are one thing; but political and economic liberties for the sake of Man in general, for Man in the skies are the substitutions of a tyrannical superstition for a genuine fact.

The Ego and his Own is well worth reading. The printers have done their best to make the book unique by printing the matter to give the appearance blank verse. The translation, however, is quite good; and, in any case, the book is far too important to be missed by anybody in search of ideas.

I've Based My Affairs on Nothing

Max Stirner
Malcom Green, translation   (1989)

There is so much that is supposed to be my business! Above all the cause of good, then God, mankind, truth, freedom, humanity and righteousness; then there is my people's cause, my prince's, and my fatherland's; and in the end there are even the affairs of the spirit and a thousand other things. Only my affairs are never supposed to be my business. "Shame on the egoist who's forever only thinking of himself!"

Let us then take a look at how the likes of them arrange their affairs, which we are supposed to work for, devote ourselves to, and feel enthusiastic about.

You are able to preach a good deal of profundity about God and have spent thousands of years "investigating the depths of the God-head" and looked into His heart, so you can certainly tell us how God Himself manages "God's affairs," which we are called upon to serve. Nor do you make any bones about the Lord's doings. But what are His affairs? Is it the same as is demanded of us? Has he made an alien cause, such as the cause of love and truth, His own? You are outraged by this misunderstanding and teach us that God's cause is naturally the cause of love and truth, and this cannot be seen as alien to Him for God Himself is love and truth. You are outraged by the assumption that God could be like us miserable worms and further a cause alien to His own. "Would God take up the cause of truth if He wasn't truth Himself?" He only cares about His affairs, but because He is the sum of all things, everything has got to be His affair! But we, we are not the sum of all things, and our affairs are quite paltry and contemptible; thus we have to serve a "higher cause." — Well, it is quite clear, God only attends to His own, is only concerned about Himself, only thinks about Himself and only has Himself in sight; woe to anything which does not find pleasure in His eyes. He serves no higher cause and satisfies only Himself. His affairs are purely egoistic ones.

How is it with humanity, whose affairs we are meant to make our own? Are humanity's affairs to any extent someone else's, does it serve a higher cause? No. Humanity only looks after itself, humanity only wishes to further humanity, humanity itself is its concern. Peoples and individuals are tormented, doing their duty for humanity, so that it can develop, and when they have achieved what humanity requires, they are cast on the scrap heap of history by way of thanks. Is it not humanity's cause a purely egoistic one?

I really do not need to go through the list of everything which wants to inflict its cause upon us in order to show that they are all only concerned with themselves, not with us, only with their own well-being, and not ours. Just take a look at the rest of them yourselves. Do truth, freedom, humanity or righteousness desire anything else than that you are aflame with enthusiasm and serve them?

They are all exceptionally full of themselves when they receive our zealous bornage. Just take a look at the nation, which is defended by devoted patriots. The patriots fall in bloody battle or in their battle with hunger or need: what does the nation care? The nation "blossoms," fertilised by their corpses! These individuals have died for "the great cause of the nation," and the nation addresses them with a parting word of thanks and — reaps the profits. That is what I call a lucrative form of egoism.

And just take a look at that sultan who lavishes so much care on "his people." Isn't he the embodiment of pure selflessness, sacrificing himself hour after hour for his people? Quite right, for "his people." Just try it some lime, show him that you are not one of his but your own boss: you'll end up strolling off to jail for absconding from his egoism. The sultan has based his cause on nothing else than himself: he is the sum of all things, the only one in his eyes, and tolerates nobody who dares to be not one of "his people."

And you do not want to learn from these dazzling examples that it is the egoist who makes the most headway? I for my part draw a lesson from them, and instead of carrying on selflessly serving these great egoists, prefer to be the egoist myself.

God's and humanity's affairs are concerned with nothing, nothing but themselves. So I shall also base my affairs on myself, my self which for others is as equally nothing as God is, my self which is my all, my self which is unique.

If, as you all assure me, both God and humanity have enough substance to be the sum of all things, then I am sure that I shall be even less lacking and will not have to bemoan my "emptiness." I am not nothing in the sense of emptiness, but am rather the creative nothingness, the nothingness on which I draw as the creator of all things.

So away with every affair which is not completely my own! You think that I should at least be concerned with the "cause of the good?" What is good, what is evil? After all I am my own cause, and I am neither good nor evil. Neither of them mean a thing to me.

The divine is God's affair, humanity's affairs are "man's." My affairs are neither divine nor human, have nothing to do with truth, goodness, justice, freedom etc., but solely with that which is mine; not general concerns but rather — unique ones, just as I am unique.

Nothing is more important than myself!

ANTHONY LUDOVICI

Anthony Ludovici (1882–1971) was a British author, translator and philosopher. He contributed to Dr. Oscar Levy's *The Complete Works of Friedrich Nietzsche* as well as several books on Nietzsche of his own. In 1906 he was the private secretary to Auguste Rodin. Ludovici served as a translator, an officer and an intelligence agent for England during World War I.

Let the views of Anthony Ludovici be told in selected titles to his books: *Who is to be Master of the World? An Introduction to the Philosophy of Friedrich Nietzsche* (1909); *A Defence of Aristocracy: A Text-Book for Tories* (1915); *Enemies of Women: the Origins in Outline of Anglo-Saxon Feminism* (1948); *The Quest of Human Quality: How to Rear Leaders* (1952); *The Specious Origins of Liberalism: The Genesis of a Delusion* (1967).

> "To hold typically liberal views, therefore, and to assume that if we liked we could all settle down to love one another and live in perfect amity and harmony together, is possible only to those idealists who are congenitally blind to the true character of all life; whilst as for those numskulls who begin to see and think of the Will to Power only when figures like Napoleon, Stalin or Hitler appear, and who overlook it wholly in themselves, their wives, their children and their cat, they are even more dangerous than the idealists aforesaid." —Anthony Ludovici, *Religion for Infidels* (London: Holborn 1961)

Portrait of Anthony Ludovici by Claude Harris, 1927.

ARTICLES IN THIS SECTION

ANTHONY M. LUDOVICI'S EGOISM
KEVIN I. SLAUGHTER   (2017)

The Union of Egoists tries to make a distinction between egoism that is explicitly inspired or intellectually descended from Max Stirner, and things that are merely egoistic. There are many people who one could say were egoists, and wrote things that were perfectly egoistic, but we have to draw lines of delineation. One of those lines is trying to keep the majority of our work within the years 1845 to 1945.

British Nietzschean elitist Anthony M. Ludovici (1882 — 1971) is not a name many modern readers would associate with egoism and Max Stirner, although I believe that is due to the narrowing of Stirner's audience to the anarchist milieu over time. It is clear Ludovici is familiar with Stirner, and Ludovici is among the earliest Americans exposed to the German's works.

Recently in doing research relating to the School of Living and Ralph Borsodi, I noticed—was shocked—to see Ludovici listed as part of an "Advisory Council" in a 1967 issue of their journal *The Way Out* (later discoveries would temper that shock, but that's for another essay). Borsodi himself was influenced by Benjamin Tucker, Friedrich Nietzsche, Henry George, Lysander Spooner, and Arthur Schopenhauer among others. Borsodi rejected the label of anarchist, though his lifelong champion Mildred Loomis did not.

In *Who is to be Master of This World? / An Introduction to the Philosophy of Friedrich Nietzsche* (London: Allen & Unwin 1909), published just two years after the first English-language edition of *The Ego and His Own*, Ludovici mentions of Stirner in discussing Nietzsche:

> From that time forward, Nietzsche began to regard our modern values "good" and "evil" with ever-increasing suspicion, and literally did not rest until he had formulated the theory expounded in his latter works. Of course we had had moralists, or preferably immoralists, who, without offering a substitute, had attacked the Christian values. French books had been plentiful, and Stirner in modern times had presented us with a strikingly original and very deep work on the subject. But the only favourable comment we find concerning any modern school of ethics, in Nietzsche's works, relates to Herbert Spencer. The position Spencer assumes,

although not sanctioned by Nietzsche, is nevertheless declared to be "psychologically tenable."

In a 1963 Ludovici essay from *The South African Observer* titled "The Essentials of Good Government," Stirner is mentioned alongside other notable figures, though not in a flattering way:

> This probably explains the frequency with which the advocates of Anarchism and newfangled policies like Socialism, Communism and other forms of State ownership of the means of production, together with all the grave errors in Psychology which these systems involve, emanate from middle-class minds; that is to say, the minds of men who have never experienced want and have in their family lines long enjoyed the safety of a well-regulated existence.
>
> From the ancient Greek, Zeno (B.C. 342 — 267), who set his community, destitute of any government, against Plato's ordered State, down to our William Godwin, the Frenchman, Proudhon, the German, Max Stirner, and men like Thoreau and Tolstoy, all these professed Anarchists have come from middle-class families, traditionally contented with their lot and belonging to a type which might be fancifully described as "Surfeited with Smugness."

Over fifty years passed between the writing of those two items. It is wise to note that more time passed between these two mentions of Max Stirner than Max Stirner was alive.

The following excerpt is from Anthony M. Ludovici's book *The Choice of a Mate* (London: John Lane, 1935). While one can discuss Ludovici's other work and its compatibility or incompatibility with egoism, the following passage cannot be disputed in its naked Stirnerite egoism. Not just vaguely egoistic, but explicit "enlightened egoism."

THE CHOICE OF A MATE (EXCERPT)
ANTHONY M. LUDOVICI   (1935)

From the very beginning it would be well for all young people to rec-
ognize that on this question of unselfishness and selfishness and the
praise and blame commonly accorded to each, Christian teaching is
psychologically false. Owing to its early appeal to the pariah and the
outcast, this religion constantly reveals a psychology framed more
on demagogic appeal than actual fact. The very command, "Love one
another!" like the Mosaic command, "Honour thy father and thy
mother," is based on a misunderstanding of normal mental processes.
Love and honour are not voluntary; they are a natural, inevitable and
quite involuntary reaction to the lovableness and honourableness of
the object, whether neighbour or parent.

No command can make one love anyone who is not lovable. "Seek
neighbours that are loveable so that you may inevitably love them,"
would have been more sensible. "Love one another!" is shallow and
reveals a poor, almost benighted grasp of human psychology. You
might just as well say, "Admire one another," or "Esteem one another."
These reactions depend on certain qualities in the other, and cannot
be auto-generated in response to a command even from a god.

The same remarks apply to the Mosaic "Honour thy father and
thy mother!" The proper command would have been: "Parents, make
yourselves honourable in the sight of your children!" I take it that all
intellectually honest persons know that in everything they do, they
act either under compulsion, from inclination, or from self-interest.
There is no such thing as a consistent course of so-called "unselfish"
conduct that is not pursued for some kind of self-gratification. Charity is the most transparent of these.

Everybody, therefore, is consistently "selfish." The wise, however,
are "enlightened egoists," i.e. they are "selfish" only up to the point
when self ceases to be best served by "selfishness," as, for instance,
in their relationship to immediate dependents who can minister
to their happiness, in their relationship to menials, retainers, and
friends, all of whom may make life happy or the reverse, for a central
figure. And the unwise are "unenlightened egoists," i.e. they carry
"selfishness" to a point which turns their environment against them,
so that, in the end, "self" gets badly served and is made unhappy as

the result of "selfishness."

The mistake is to suppose that the "enlightened egoist" is "unselfish," and that the "unenlightened egoist" is "selfish." Both are "selfish" —if the word has any meaning at all, but whereas the former is so with intelligence, the latter is so as a dolt and dullard.

Anthony Ludovici

DORA MARSDEN

In 1908 Dora joined and became a leader in the Women's Social and Political Union (WPSU). The following year she resigned as a teacher and became a full-time agitator for the WSPU. She was sentenced to two months in prison for vandalism in 1909. After a hunger strike she was released and continued to agitate and disrupt political meetings (including a speech by a young Winston Churchill).

In 1911, Dora founded *The Freewoman* (1911 – 1912). Financial troubles led to a re-launch as *The New Freewoman* (1914). An ever-more keen search for liberty led to a re-launch as *The Egoist* (1914 – 1919).

In the 1920s – 1930s Dora wrote three books: *The Definition of the Godhead* (1928), *The Mysteries of Christianity* (1930) and *The Philosophy of Time* (published only in 1955). During the writing of these books she went from a self-imposed isolation to confinement in a mental hospital, where she spent the remainder of her life.

> "There is only one person concerned in the freeing of individuals: and that is the person who wears and feels and resents the shackles. Shackles must be burst off: if they are cut away from outside, they will immediately reform." — Dora Marsden, *The Freewoman* Vol. 1 No. 1 (June 15 1913)

Dora Marsden under arrest 1909.

ARTICLES IN THIS SECTION

Under the heading "Cassandra and the War," the *Philadelphia Evening Public Ledger* for January 6th 1915 quotes Dora Marsden speaking about World War I from *The Egoist* Volume I Number 19 (October 1 1914). Dora's background was that of a suffragette, one of the star agitators of the Women's Political Suffrage Union. The WPSU held that nothing in the world was more important than the women's vote, and that a women's vote would bring about a heretofore unseen era of peace, prosperity and equality. When the War to End All Wars began, the Women's Political Suffrage Union announced a pause in their campaign to obtain the vote for women. They stopped publishing their newspaper *The Suffragette*, and began publishing a nationalist newspaper called *Britannia*. Dora was by this time supportive neither of voting nor of nations, but of the powerful, self-responsible individual. Cassandra was a woman who rejected the advances of the god Apollo, who blessed her with the gift of prophecy coupled with the curse that no one would believe her. This fate drove her mad. Dora doubted women's suffrage would bring about a heretofore unseen era of peace, prosperity and equality. She, too, found her fate, but the reader is invited to count the wars and disparities that suffrage of any breed seems yet to resolve.

Errata for *Definition of the Godhead* by Dora Marsden.

The Egoist was the third magazine published by Dora Marsden (1882 — 1960), preceded by *The New Freewoman* and before that *The Freewoman*. This advertisement first published in *The Little Review* Volume IV Number 4 (August 1917). *The Egoist* began the serialization of *Ulysses* by James Joyce and *The Little Review* completed it. Ezra Pound was published in both magazines as well. *Lingual Psychology / The Science of Signs* by Dora Marsden appeared in serial form in *The Egoist*.

Reprinted from *The Egoist* Volume 1 Number 5 (March 2nd, 1914). Dora makes reference to the German economist Walter Eucken (1891 – 1950) and to the titled socialists Martha Beatrice Webb (1858 – 1943) and Sidney Webb (1859 – 1947).

Dora Marsden's England
Trevor Blake

(2018)

A chronological list of some of the places Dora Marsden lived, worked and published. The year listed is a year Dora was known to be there, not necessarily the first or only year Dora was there. Understandably, some locations are much changed since her time. Address is followed by approximate latitude / longitude. The map shown here features the location of the first meeting of the Freewoman Discussion Circle as shown on a map from the time.

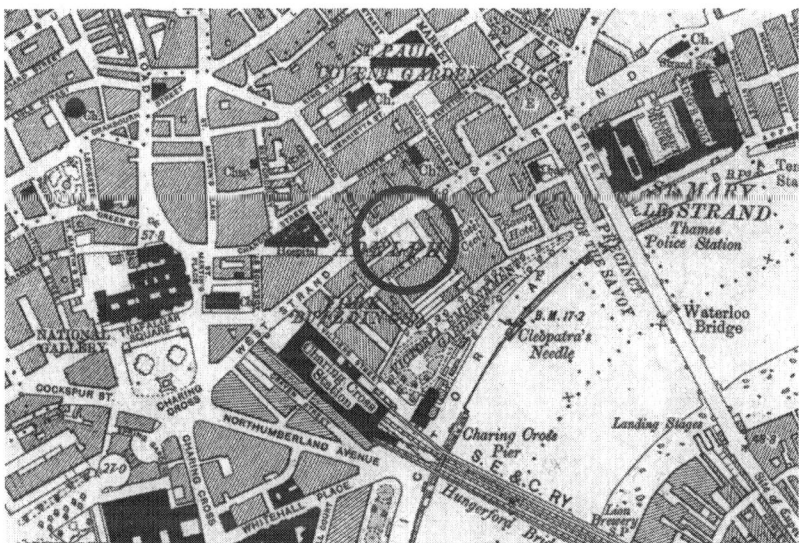

The Hey (1882)
Birthplace
1 Hey Cottages, Waters Road, Marsden,
Huddersfield, HD7 6NJ, UK
53.604199 / -1.946344

Crow Hill (1890)
Residence
Crow Hill Lodge, Carrs Rd, Marsden, Huddersfield HD7 6JH, UK
53.600526 / -1.919391

210 Greame St (1900)
Residence
210 Greame St, Manchester M14, UK
53.455111 / -2.238713

University of Manchester, formerly Victoria University (1900)
Employment
Oxford Rd, Manchester, M13 9PL, UK
53.464077 / -2.231485

Pankhurst Centre (1903)
WPSU Founded
60-62 Nelson Street, Chorlton on Medlock,
Manchester, M13 9WP, UK
53.463164 / -2.227364

26 Gathorne Terrace (1903)
Residence
26 Gathorne Terrace, Leeds LS8, UK
53.81368 / -1.5233

HM Prison Holloway (1909)
Prison
Parkhurst Rd, London N7 0NU, UK
51.555483 / -0.122028

London Road Brigton Station (1909)
Celebration of Dora's release from HM Prison Holloway
Brighton BN1 6BZ, UK
50.836667 / -0.136389

141 Chorlton Road (1909)
Residence
141 Chorlton Rd, Manchester M15, UK
53.46387 / -2.25796

Empire Hall (1909)
Dora confronts Churchhill
7 Packer Street, Rochdale, Greater Manchester, OL16 1NJ, UK
53.615937 / -2.157473

HM Prison Manchester (Strangeways) (1909)
Prison
1 Southall St, Manchester M60 9AH, UK
53.491981 / -2.246167

22 Grove Place (1911)
Residence
22 Grove Pl, Hampstead, London NW3 1JP, UK
51.559246 / -0.17568

The Freewoman (1911)
First office
9 John St, London WC1N 2ES, UK
51.521999 / -0.115064

International Woman's Suffrage Shop (1911)
Freewoman Discussion Circle preliminary meeting and first meeting
15 Adam St, London WC2N 6RJ, UK
51.509765 / -0.122525

The Freewoman (1912)
Printer
4 Kirby Grove, London, UK
51.519764 / -0.107036

The Freewoman (1912)
Second office
16 King Street, Covent Garden, London, WC2E 8JF, UK
51.511347 / -0.124847

Chandos Hall (1912)
Freewoman Discussion Circles second and remaining meetings
Granby Row, Manchester M1 3QJ, UK
53.475529 / -2.234765

"The Hey" (1912)
Residence
Hatfield Rd, Southport PR8 2PE, UK
53.605536 / -3.042869

The New Freewoman (1912)
Office
61 Riding House Street London W1W 7EQ, UK
51.519287 / -0.139161

9 Hatfield Rd (1913)
Residence
9 Hatfield Rd, Southport PR8 2PE, UK
53.604738 / -3.042083

Seldom Seen (1920)
Residence
Glenridding, Penrith, CA11 0QT, UK
54.544836 / -2.949773

Chrichton Royal Hospital (1935)
Hospital
Grierson House, Bankend Rd, Dumfries DG1 4ZE, UK
55.05038 / -3.590817

Dora Marsden

CASSANDRA AND THE WAR
UNCREDITED (1915)

It is quite a different phase of the war that Dora Marsden presents in a gloomy and foreboding prophecy. Miss Marsden, once prominent in settlement and suffrage work, "advanced" out of that stage to founding a very radical weekly, *The Freewoman*. Current opinion quotes the following from a recent article of hers in *The Egoist*, another radical English weekly:

> The war — still the war — has brought the wordy contest about women's rights to an abrupt finish, and only a few sympathetic words remain to be spoken over the feminist corpse.
>
> Every form of self-responsible power demands – not the last, the first – capable physical self-defense. One might venture to say it would be impossible to find in these islands any "advanced" woman who has not felt herself made into something of a fool by the unequivocal evidence as to the position of women presented by the war, not merely in the countries actually devastated by the war, here in England. They find that they may busy themselves with efforts to protect their less "protected" sisters; they may have the honor of being allowed to share in their country's defense by dint of knitting socks; or serve, as one ungalant soldier put it, by providing one of the "horrors of war" as a Red Cross nurse. In the war area itself they form part, along with the rest of the property, of the spoils of the conquered. One cannot easily refrain from the inference that, though they have weakened the pull of the old-womanly competence, the "advanced women" have done very little in the way of furnishing the necessary foundations for its successor.

To the Great Name Hushed Among Us for So Long
Errata for *Definition of the Godhead* by Dora Marsden
Trevor Blake   *(2018)*

Dora Marsden was the editor of *The Freewoman* (1911-1912), *The New Freewoman* (1913) and *The Egoist* (1914-1918). Dora demanded everything from those around her, generally giving little in return. She alienated her feminist readers with her egoism, she turned in her work late and she demanded changes after she'd turned over her copy to the printer. Antagonizing the printer for *The Freewoman* was why she had to re-launch the journal as *The New Freewoman*, and again as *The Egoist*. Antagonizing her friends was why she stepped down as editor after printing *The Egoist* Volume 1 Number 13 (July 1st, 1919). Dora was not able to work with her friend Harriet Weaver Shaw, and so she turned *The Egoist* over to Shaw to spend time writing books.

The first book she wrote was *The Definition of the Godhead*. Margaret Storm Jameson took the manuscript for this book to numerous publishers, all of whom rejected it. With not one drop of pride swallowed, Dora took the book to Shaw. Perhaps out of respect for better times between them, Shaw agreed to publish the book. *The Definition of the Godhead* was issued on December 1st, 1928. Five hundred copies were printed, one hundred of which were bound. The bound copies are in blue cloth, 8vo and are 390 pages. Jameson sent copies of *The Definition of the Godhead* out for review. Aside from neutral mentions of the 'books received' variety, there were three reviews (*The New Age*, the *Times Literary Supplement* and *Congregational Quarterly*), all far from flattering. Jameson offered the book for sale in her own bookstore. A total of six copies sold.

Dora wrote *The Mysteries of Christianity* in 1930, also published by The Egoist Press. In 1935 she was committed as a mental patient to Crichton Royal Hospital, where she would live until her death in 1960. A medical record of May 1st, 1948 reads: "This little lady sits quietly in her chair all day, most of the time absorbed in her own thoughts. She never mixes with the others. Reads the paper then does some sewing. She still retains the highest opinion of her own work — the last her magnum opus, two volumes of which have been published and five volumes in transcript... The patient regards them as her soul and very precious." In 1955, Shaw once again came to the aid of her old friend and published Dora's third and final book, *The Philosophy of Time.*

I own Margaret Storm Jameson's copy of *The Definition of the Godhead*, signed and inscribed by Dora Marsden. I have also closely examined another copy of *The Definition of the Godhead*. Both of these copies include annotations by Dora throughout. Dora was simply not able to let her books be written, they were eternally in the process of being written.

The Definition of the Godhead includes two entries of Errata following numbered page 390. These were changes Dora made as the book was being published, changes made close enough to the time of publication that they are bound into the book itself. Both my copy and the observed copy also have a laid in sheet of Additional Errata. The Additional Errata sheets are in two states, the shorter list likely preceding the longer list. The two versions of Additional Errata are first identified here, and they are referred to as First State and Second State. The shorter list, in the copy I observed, is here identified as Additional Errata First State. The longer list, in the copy I own, is here identified as Additional Errata Second State. There is no point of issue in the book itself distinguishing a First or Second State. Instead, the State is determined by the Additional Errata sheet laid in. Those who prefer earlier editions will prefer the First State, those who prefer authoritative editions will prefer the Second State. Here are the two Additional Errata sheets. There is no explanation for why Dora repeated some of the errata, such as "for *frankly* read *frankly*."

Additional Errata (First State)

Page 20, line 20. For *need* read *was*
Page 153, note 1. For *Eusebus* read *Eusebis*
Page 209, line 8. For *Parmendides* read *Parmenides*
Page 223, line 40. Delete comma after *being*
Page 227, last line of text. Insert reference number 2 after dismissed
Page 240, line 18. For *which, adopted by Philo* read *adopted by*

Philo, which
Page 262, line 11. For *that* read *as*
Page 263, line 25. For *fragment* read *fragments*
Page 318, line 1. For *profession* read *profusion*
Page 320, line 1. For *unto* read *into*
Page 378, line 3. For *except* read *expect*

Additional Errata (Second State)

Page 20, line 20. For *need* read *was*
Page 46, line 37. For *outselves* read *ourselves*
Page 61, line 32. For *divisions* read *dimensions*
Page 69, line 31. For *Tau* read *theta*
Page 74, line 11. For *its* read *a*
Page 116, line 12. For *essense* read *essence*
Page 121, line 31. For *of* read *on*
Page 126, line 8. For *is* read *is*
Page 133, line 8. Delete half-bracket
Page 147, line 1. For *their* read *its*
Page 149, line 26. For *Heracleitan* read *Heracleitean*
Page 153, line 11. For *is* read *gives*
Page 153, note 1. For *Eusebus* read *Eusebius*
Page 160, line 4. For *movement,* read *movement.*
Page 164, line 11. For *such* read the *most*
Page 209, line 8. For *Parmendides* read *Parmenides*
Page 223, line 40. Delete comma after being,
Page 227, line 28. Insert reference number 2 after dismissed
Page 240, line 18. For *which, adopted by Philo* read *adopted by Philo, which*
Page 263, line 25. For *fragment* read *fragments*
Page 272, line 12. For *that* read *as*
Page 318, line 1. For *profession* read *profusion.*
Page 320, line 1. For *unto* read *into*
Page 360, line 29. For *frankly* read *frankly*
Page 378, line 3. For *except* read *expect*

Additional Errata First State has eleven entries while Additional

Errata Second State has twenty-six entries. Unique to Additional Errata First State is "Page 262, line 11. For that read as." The passage reads: "That is, we contend that the infinite causal regress Aristotle [has in mind is not only an impossibility but is an inescapable necessity]." The passage is unchanged in both copies. It could be that Dora came to accept her word choice as published and removed this First State entry from Second State. Shared but at variance between First State and Second State are "Page 223, line 40. Delete comma after being" (Second State adds a final comma) and "Page 160, line 4. For movement; read movement" (Second State adds a final period). "Page 126, line 8. For is read is" appears to mean change the italic as published to plain text.

Miscellaneous Annotations

The annotations Dora wrote in *The Definition of the Godhead* generally follow the Additional Errata and consist of a word crossed out with an alternative word written in. But sometimes Dora would annotate the book in variance to the printed Errata. The First State includes the following annotations which are not in any Additional Errata.

Page 39, line 14. "or" crossed out, "of" written in.
Page 44, line 8. the final letter of "terms" crossed out, question mark in left margin.
Page 75, line 23. "and" crossed out, "or" written in.
Page 102, line 31. arrow pointing to "we."
Page [108], final two lines. "there can be no permanently binding conception of the Godhead" is underlined.
Page 109, first three lines. Bracket in left margin.
Page [140], lines beginning "world-sorters" and "(holy)". Line of emphasis in left margin.
Page [150], line 7. "unitary 'Space-Time' is erroneous" is underlined.
Page [150], line 19. "what" is underlined, line of emphasis in left margin.
Page [150], line 22. "who" is underlined.
Page 194, footnote. Line of emphasis in left margin.
Page 227, footnote. Line of emphasis in left margin; "our ten-

dency to take uncritically the teachings of the great Greeks: of Plato in particular" is underlined.

Page 228, line 16. Checkmark in left margin.

Page 249, line 37. "Space" crossed out; line to bottom margin; ""It is the construction which this philosopher Gas[sendi] or Newton's gravitational theory which has been omitted from appendix i; which, as stated, his views are Space." p. 391" written in.

Page 262, line 11. "that" crossed out, "as" written in.

Page 263, lines 25 through 30. Line of emphasis in left margin.

Page 287, footnote. "Gilbert himself absolutely disregarded authority, and accepted nothing at second hand" is underlined; lines beginning "and repeated" and "experiment" line of emphasis left margin.

Page 297, footnote. Checkmark in left margin next to line beginning "of Time."

Dora references Pierre Gassendi (1592 – 1655) in her marginalia on page 249. Gassendi was a French priest and mathematician, known for being the first person to view the transit of a planet across the face of the sun. It is not known which book by or about Gassendi Dora was referencing with her notation of "p[age] 391."

The Egoist Advertised
in *The Little Review*   *(1917)*

ANENT THE DECALOGUE
DORA MARSDEN (1914)

Perhaps the most striking illustration of the unquestioning habit of mind common to us all is the tone in which we use the word "immoral." Actions may be all things else and be tolerated, but if they are voted "immoral" their case is closed: they are damned, though most of us would need to be hard-pressed before we were able to say why. For obviously all that is said when one says "immoral" is "not-customary." It is informing to note moreover that while not-customary conduct is to be damned, it in nowise follows that its positive opposite is to be blessed. People are not prepared to admire enthusiastically "customary conduct": they have in fact no very high opinion of it: why then the working up of fierce indignation at the prospect of its contrary? That the "faithful" have been aware of the difficulty is shown by the extensive searches they have made to find the justification of "moral" conduct both as to foundations and superstructure: what inquiry into the Fundamentals of Ethics has shown to be missing the Metaphysics of Morals has attempted to make good. Indeed to enjoy the spectacle of human beings indulging in the full tide of talk in their least graceful moments one must turn to them when they are presenting the "philosophy" of morals. On no other occasions do they twist, shift and cant with so little effect of grace. And they are still hard at it and still stick at nothing. If moral conduct does not suit men, then change the men. The latest Defender of the Sacred, Eucken, unconsciously puts their case neatly. He says:

Before all else the natural world keeps man bound down to the mere ego; it becomes clearly visible that, as compared with the strength of the mere man, something impossible is being demanded. Therefore man must become something more than mere man. The original affirmation has become intolerable, but out of the negation has arisen a new affirmation. Here are great demands and great upheavals, gigantic tides of life sweeping men along and transforming them... an inner infinitude becomes increasingly manifest. If anything can show us that our life is not a matter of indifference, that in it something significant takes place, it is morality that can do it.

"Moral" conduct is, as its name implies, "customary" conduct. Its advantages are the advantages of all repetitive action which is facile and foreseeable because habituated. Moral conduct is mechanised conduct and possesses all the advantages of mechanical reliability. It fits almost perfectly on to the routineer. Its disadvantages are the same: it plays havoc when it comes into contact with the new and unexpected: meets the unobserved factor which was not taken account of in blocking out the moral plan. To fit properly, moral conduct would need to be the activity of a "living automaton" — of a combination of forces which are denials of each other. It is the conjoining of these two contradictions which enables men to construct "tragedy." The recipe for the production of a Tragedy, i.e. a play upon a simulated Terror, is as follows: A collection of living beings with an appetite for experience, adventurous therefore; a recognition of a species of conduct customary to the people to which the special collection belongs (what species of course being quite immaterial); lastly a "respect" for the second in the "intellect" of the first. These three ingredients mixed well together will account for any of the "great tragedies" known to men. Every "tragedy" has a "problem": playwrights spin their brains to shreds to concoct one: a new "problem" will win fame for any playwright: so anxious are men to enjoy the sensation of mock Terror: the so-called purgation through pity and horror. To understand the fascination of "Tragedy" it is necessary to realise that all Tragedy is melodrama, that is: actual living judged by a "concept" of living. It is worked by dint of an acceptance of the hoisting of a sky-scape, a canvas stretched across the mental heavens whereon is painted the moral scheme to which the herd below make effort to comport themselves. The "tragedy" is achieved by concentrating attention on the movements of those who being the least herd-like venture to ignore the sky-scape in order to follow their own bent for experience, thereby inviting the onslaughts of the terror-stricken herd. If the playwright can make it look feasible for the "hero" himself to participate in the herd's horror at his "sacrilege" the chances of success are heightened, the "heinous" effect of the situation upon which the "Terror" of the tragedy depends thereby having been increased.

The effect of tragedy on an appreciative audience appears to be a subconscious one. Of a certainty its effect is not what Aristotle said was the function of these representations of woes of heroes — "to purge the mind by pity and terror of these and similar emotions." The unconscious effect of tragedy is to reveal as the slang phrase has it "the greatness of man" as against the cobweb-like mesh of "thoughts" to which men lend the moulding of their actions as an affair of sport and make believe. Melodrama purges terror of its basis of terror: as the turning up of a light in a dark room at once makes an object which in the half-light looked fearsome and strange, obvious and harmless. Those most swayed by concepts relish "tragedy" most. They enjoy it because subconsciously they are ceasing to respect the reality of the concepts which are the making of it. Melodrama because it displays in so garish a light the nature of "morals" is the subtlest sapping of the framework it is built on: which accounts for the unfriendliness of advocates of the sacred for this attractive but too destructively bright exhibition of their holy ghosts-the moral concepts. The churches for instance cannot be friendly towards drama: half-tones are among the foremost of the churches' exigences. So too, it is obvious that the arch-conceptualist, Plato, must demand the rigorous suppression of tragedy in his model republic.

It is clear that the one emotion which the moralists cannot afford to permit to weaken is: Fear. (They would call it reverence, but no matter.) Whatever strengthens human fear is to them the basis of "good": because "Fear" is disintegrating, and throws its owner in submission on to the breast of any and every concept which is thrust forward and called "salvation." The moralists exploit and play upon the feeling of smallness and loneliness which is the first outcome of that sense of isolation and separateness which is called self-consciousness. It is because men are in the first place lonely and afraid, that the feebler sort move in herds and act alike: hence the growth of "customary" action: moral action. The outcry against the "immoral," i.e. the unusual, is the expression of distress of the timid in the presence of the innovation. It is the instinct which feels there is safety with the crowd and danger as well as loneliness in adventuring individually which puts the poignant note into the epithet "immoral." To be "immoral" is to be on precisely the same level as the unconventional and the unfashionable: that and no more.

Although "morals," i.e. the collective term applied to automatised action, are based on the all-too-commonly observable phenomenon that the actions of herds at a given time run to one pattern, in the course of time it is a patent fact that certain influences acting on the herds tend to change the pattern. "Fashions" give the best illustration of how "morals" change. When crinolines for instance are "in," all women wear crinolines; when they are "out," to wear a crinoline would be a mild scandal, but something else is "in," and all women like sheep are approximating to that. So with "morals." They change but when they do the herd changes with them as by a common impulse. It is therefore only on account of the little extravagances of the rhetoricians — who will do many things to come by a good sounding mouthful — that we hear talk of "the changeless law of morality." Morals are fashions in conduct that are constantly changing: but change as they will they will find their faithful attendant crowd of timorous and ineffectuals. The strong and alert are never moral: when they appear upon occasion to be so, it is by mere coincidence. It is the realisation of this fact that they are catering only for the needs of the feeble which puts zest into the ambitions of great "founders," "leaders," "teachers." They can lay down precepts fit for followers with easy minds because it is only the born followers that will follow. So each new "leader" has his "precept" for the guidance of the faithful: the "pattern" according to which they must work. Each "New Dispensation" has its "law," and it would be a pity to leave the precepts of the decalogue without turning over the commandment of the newest dispensation which in a curiously odd way has worked itself haphazard in and among the pattern of the older which still verbally holds good.

The commandment "Love one another" is an advance in subtlety as compared with the injunctions it was intended to supersede. It is an attempt to establish an intra-conscious police in the shape of Conscience. It is what the Webbs for instance would call a move in the direction of "efficiency in administration," as the spy-system is more "efficient" than an ordinary police-system. More efficient because more intimate, and more effective because it is easy to control actions once feeling has been surrendered under control. The favour with which the command to "Love one another" was received is evidence of the strength of the desire for neighbourly espionage and democratic control of "each by all" of which all modern legislation is but the grotesque parody in action. (Now with democracy merely an infant, "loving one another" only mildly, we control each other in the realms of marrying, being born, housed, clothed, educated, fed and similar minor matters only. When all "Love one another" with zeal our inter-neighbourly control will begin to show something of what it can be.)

It is therefore quite clear what motives of economy would operate in the point of view of "Authority" in substituting "compulsory love" for "compulsory circumspect behaviour" such as the decalogue enjoins. If only universal "loving" could be made the fashionable habit, the supreme "moral," how easy the work of "leaders" would be. When individuals love one another how easily they work together: how they appear successful in overcoming the otherwise unmanageable ego. Then why not make love among the herd compulsory: and hey presto: the New Dispensation: the Christian era.

How grotesque a failure and how offensive, the pose of "love according to conscience" has been no one need pause to state with the history of two thousand years written before them. Of all the attitudes which men have struck in emulation of painted canvases which have been stretched across the heavens for their guidance, none has given such good cause for individualist contempt as this. As long as conceptualists in the interest of their large concepts press only thoughts into service, the strain is little felt. But "love" is not a thought. It is worthwhile, in face of revivalist efforts in the cult of love such as, for instance, in the "gospel" of Tolstoy, to consider what people seek in those aspects of love which are not "sex": in the passionate friendships and tenderness of love: the wider emotional needs which have made their appearance with the intensification of "culture." The irony of the efforts of the advocates of the new dispensation to press "love" into the service of the "moral concepts" is not immediately apparent. It is customary to regard "love" as the outcome of "culture" and therefore in some special way amenable to the service of culture. It has become too much a habit of speech with the "civilised" world, i.e. the moralised idea-ised world, to look on "love" as in some sort a means of "salvation," to expect it to analyse why it does so. If it did men would realise that the explanation is the reverse of the current one, i.e. that love is the consummation of moralisation. It is in fact an effort to escape from it. The heavy incrustation of habitualised actions, i.e. morals, increases in tenacity as life goes on, forming a sort of hutch which is half shelter and half tomb. The taking on of its earlier incrustations is called "growing-up": as they grow more obviously oppressive it is called "growing old." To be "morally-minded" is to have lost the instinct which revolts against this walling-up of the changing spirit: revolts that is against either growing up or growing old. As most people are morally-minded the world is left with a tiny remnant of individuals of whom if we spoke of them in terms of time-measurement we should say ranged in age from two years to five: the people of genius and charm. The age of maturity, if we may put it like that, when all that we mean is the age at which the soul has made itself familiar with its new dwelling-place and is at its best, brightest, most inquiring and "true," is from two years to five: not twenty-five or fifty-five as the moralist would like to pretend. From five onwards the browbeating process which is called moral education begins, and as we have said only spirits which are bigger and more resistant than their would-be instructors resist it and stand firm at their height of growth. The rest are slowly driven back by "culture" to the state of automatic living which was their pre-natal existence. The irony therefore of the moralists' efforts to capture "love" in the interest of their already too successful canvases lies in this: that in seeking after the "tendencies" of love and the "understanding" of friendship the morally-bound individuals are seeking a refuge free from the attitudes which make them grown-up. Because they cannot appear what but for fear and a brow-beating education they would be: i.e. unashamedly children, they have tried to build a refuge in "love." The tenderness of love or friendship (they are in fact the same thing) are the instinctive means which we seek for ourselves and offer to others, to enable us, in one relation at least to be unashamedly ourselves, very little removed from new born children. This is the reason why the efforts of those of the "love-cult" to "ennoble" love appear — and appear so particularly to the quite ordinary conventional person — so irredeemably damned. To introduce an attitude into a relation whose very existence is a revolt against attitudes is to snatch from the conventional what is literally his one means of salvation, and that none too certain. It is a sufficiently rare thing for one individual to meet another with enough native sympathy with him to encourage him to show "himself," with all his weakness. It is inevitable that what we feel to be ourselves should in comparison with the harsh-set incrustations of our normal "moral" attitudes, appear "weak." The fact is overlooked that as long as the "weak" thing is there, we are still alive: and that only when the genius in us has flickered out: when we have become one with the herd, do we feel strong in our moral worth.

It is natural that "love" should have attracted the attention of the most thoroughgoing types of moralists, the churchmen or such moralists as the feminine theorisers who call themselves oddly the Woman Movement. The more powerful the agent, the more admirable if pressed into their service. It is unfortunate-for them-that in all cases where "love" has been utilised to further a "system" it has turned and gnawed a yawning gap in the system. But that is part of another story. The fact remains that the chief value of the law of the New Dispensation "Love one another" has been to make evident to men that they will have to, willy-nilly, dispense with all dispensations: that there exists for them no "grace" to be "dispensed" which they have not first called up from within themselves. And with the passing of the set manner of "dealing in grace" which is "dispensation," there passes the ghostly basis of mechanised action: "duty" and "morality"; and men begin unashamedly to judge the quality of life by its flavour in actual living: by their own "taste" in regard to it, forming thereby their principle as to what they accept and what they reject in it, which is living by a "principle of taste" — a principle which is no principle. It is living according to personal desire: life according to whim: life without principle: the essentially immoral life.

Dora Marsden

DORA MARSDEN AND THE POWER OF THOUGHT
N. C. CRITCHER *(1913)*

There could be no more forcible illustration of the power of thought than is to be so clearly seen in the wonderful change in the last few years, in the position of woman and her relation to the economic world. Not so very many years ago she was considered necessary, indeed, to the life of the world, as its reproducer, and as wife, mother, housekeeper, etc., but as completely subservient to man. This condition she almost universally accepted as her normal position. To be a good and faithful wife and mother; to be a good and obedient servant, if such were her lot, (when she happened to be a God-fearing woman,) she considered her highest duty and pleasure.

When her married life proved unfortunate, and her trials more than she could endure, divorce was open to her, to be sure, but with the penalty of social ostracism, added to the loss of her children, usually. [...]

The "new" woman is found in Turkey, in Persia, India, and Egypt, playing her part in politics in a way that would surprise American men; the *coup d'etat* by which Abdul Hamid was removed, and Mehmet V. elevated in his place, having owed much to her cooperation. And "today members of the fair sex belonging to the most exclusive families in Constantinople, are selling flowers on the street to raise money for the sufferers from the earthquake which a short time ago devastated the eastern portion of the Ottoman Empire." They are conspicuous as authors as well. In Persia's recent crisis women aided materially, as shown by Morgan Shuster, in his book, *The Strangling of Persia*.

To gain an adequate idea of the progress made by Mohammedan women, one should read the article in the December Review of Reviews, by Saint Nihal Singh. In the same magazine is another article entitled "Feminism's New Prophetess;" in which Dora Marsden, editress of the *Freewoman*, is presented in that role. She does, indeed, take a step farther into the future than even the suffragists, insisting that woman shall free herself from all traditional relations, and take her position as an "individual;" as absolutely "free spiritual entities." How far she carries her argument is not shown, but so far as stated there is nothing to startle Koreshans, whose education on those lines is far in advance of the world's present standpoint.

Are Brains Necessary?

The Koreshan Unity will open Meetings, beginning Sunday Evening, July 19, 1903, to continue Every Sunday till further notice.

KORESH SPEAKS

At Corinthian Hall, 17th Floor, Masonic Temple.

Subject, July 19:—Brains the Basis of Mental Science, and How Utilized for the Healing of Disease. Opportunity will be given for Five-Minute Criticisms after the lecture.

Lecture Begins at 7:45 p. m.

COME AND BE HEALED

"Without Money and Without Price." You are free to call in your friends to the fountain of vigor and of perpetual youth. When Jesus healed he did not make a Millionaire of himself and call it Christian Science.

Complimentary. This Admits Bearer and Friend.

Handbill for lecture series held by Cyrus Teed's Koreshan Unity.

MALFEW SEKLEW

Sirfessor F. W. Wilkesbarre (aka Malfew Seklew) was born in Great Britain in the 1860s. In the 1890s and early 1900s he was a contributor to and associate editor to *The Eagle and The Serpent*. Sirfessor came to the United States in 1916. He shared an address with Ragnar Redbeard in Chicago in 1927, the year he wrote *The Gospel According to Malfew Seklew*. By the 1930s he was living in New York City. He died in 1938.

> Are you a Simpoleon or a Supercrat? A Peter-pantheist or a Personality? Are you a Bromide or a Sulphide? A nonentity or a reality? Are you an unripe ego or an unfinished organism with underdone understanding and hard boiled beliefs, pingpong principles and petrified prejudices? Do you amble through the atmosphere with the courage of a carrot, the consciousness of a cabbage, the turpitude of a turnip, the pep of a prune, the punch of a parsnip and the psychology of a Sundowner in the swamps of Hobohemia, or do you dash through space with the courage of a Conqueror and the wisdom of a Will-to-Power Man? If not, massage your Mentoids, and be saved—from yourself at your worst.
>
> —Sirfessor F. W. Wilkesbarre,
> *The Gospel According to Malfew Seklew*

Richard G McKnight and F. M. Wilkesbarr, aka Malfew Seklew (see page 127).
Phoo circa 1927. Care of the Labadie Collection.

ARTICLES IN THIS SECTION

Malfew Seklew emerged as an evangelist not of the ego, but of atheism. His earliest work appears in *The Freethinker* in 1898, and the *Edinburg Evening News* reports his exposition on the topic in 1902. Sirfessor Seklew defended the Bradford Truthseekers in the *Burnley Express* in 1905, and protested the imprisonment (for blasphemy!) of J. W. Gott in 1911. But by the year of this remarkable essay from *The People's Press* Volume 12 Number 39 (December 11th, 1909), Malfew Seklew was also a celebrant of the self and an anti-socialist, as seen in his 1909 pamphlet *J. Bruce Glasier / Demi-Gods Demi-Damned, or Halo's Hoodooed*. Seklew speaks softly of the proletariat and the workers, a contradiction signaling his transition from unconscious to conscious egoist had yet to be completed. But like every other *Ignis Fatuus* — phantom, illusion — pining for the progress of the poor will soon slip from the speech of Seklew. Our hero never appears again in *The People's Press*.

Will Crooks (1852 – 1921) grew up in a poor house and engaged in labor for most of his life. When he spoke up as a labor organizer and later a politician, his expressions came from experience and not expediency. In the following uncredited article from the *Kentish Independent* for Friday 29 July 1904, Mr. Crooks lends his credibility to an organization organized by street sellers (or costers), registered number 1,336. Among them is Mr. F. Wilkesbarre. The evening's entertainment also included a film from Ruffle's Imperial Bioscope, producers of the lost films *Dealers in Human Lives*, *The Kiss of Hate* and *Locked in Death*.

A simple series of shills from Sirfessor Seklew. A handsome reward is offered to the first to step forward and offer for sale any of the sacred artifacts described in *Der Geist*.

John William Gott (1866 – 1922) was an atheist orator and associate of Sirfessor Malfew Seklew. In 1903 he took part in a charity debate with a theist in the club room of the local Independent Labor Party (ILP). The press later reported Gott did not hold up his end of the debate, and our man Malfew set him straight in the following letter to the editor in the *Bradford Daily Telegraph* Volume LXXI Number 10,709 (February 29th, 1903) page 3. In 1922, Gott was the last person to be sent to prison in Britain for blasphemy.

THE REJECTION OF CHRISTIANITY
MALFEW SEKLEW (1909)

I reject Christianity because it is the evangel of self-abnegation instead of self-assertion — also because it glorifies Altruism, Duty, Humility, Submission, Contentment and other slave virtues.

I believe Christianity to be the cause of the decadence of the common people, and, for the existence of this respectable barbarism, erroneously described as "civilization."

Civilization is not worth having, where the wants of the individual are not satisfied. For what is civilization if it bring not happiness? For this I reject Christianity.

I reject Christianity because I think — with Government — it is responsible for this pseudo-civilization with its corroding charity, its cant, hypocrisy, wage slavery, the sybaritic splendor of the parasites and the squalid misery of the producer. I reject it because it is founded on a myth, build 'round a neurotic nonentity — like Santa Claus — who never lived except in the diseased imagination of hare-brained hierarchs, deluded decadents, persons suffering from hypothetical nebulosity, and a few others who are afflicted with sympathetic diarrhea. I believe Christianity is a curse, an incubus on the minds of the mutable many, a nightmare of nastinesss consisting of hoary hobgoblins, ghouls, ghosts, gore and gluttony. For this I reject it.

Christianity breeds myriads of cretinous creatures. In the churches — those intellectual opium joints — can be seen sophisticated sycophantic sky pilots — navigating to a land not on the map — Pharisees, sterilized Sadducees and subordinated sucklings.

These last mentioned benighted and bedamned bipeds seem content with a hell while on earth, for the expectation of having a hell of a time in heaven. Poor, pure, putrid persons!

I repudiate Christianity and all other theorems that quall under the stern, staunch, steadfast gaze of reason and scientific analysis. I reject it because its devotees have ever been the enemies of progress and the proletariat; because it is founded on fiction, not fact — blindfolded belief, not judgement, knowledge or reason. Christianity has strenuously striven to uphold the Trinity of Damnation, those malefactors of Mankind, God, Government, and Grundy, and has even been the foe of those Benefactors — Liberty, Learning and Love.

I reject it because it demoralizes the minds of the demi-damned — the workers; chloroforms the conceptions of womankind, and confuses and confounds the brains of the young. I reject it absolutely, now, to-day, to-morrow and the day after, because I do not want to burst a blood vessel — and die young — chasing an *Ignis Fatuus*. In fact, I would rather associate with the Devil — the one the Christians are so much afraid of — than murder the microbes in the atmosphere, with monotonous music, sitting on the throne of heaven as the Left Bower of Jesus. Rather would I frizzle forever in the fiery flames of Phlegethon with a rollicking roving rascal like the Devil for a companion than mercilessly masticate celestial ether, singing hosannahs to measly-mouthed, meek-eyed, mentally maimed mannikins like Jesus H. Christ, or doing the hero worshiping act, glorifying that impotent impossibility, Jehovah.

Christianity is the gospel for rainbow chasers, snobocrats, sucklings, slaves and sycophants, not for mortals who need neither God nor Master. I reject it because it is a Pot-Pourri of pain, punishment, pruriency, putridity and paralogy.

MR. F. WILKESBARRE, COSTER
UNCREDITED   (1904)

The Costers' Union. / Unfurling The Banner. /
Last Night's Proceedings.

Last night (Thursday) Barnard's Theatre Royal, Woolwich, was crowd-ed at both performances, great interest being manifested in the un-furling of the banner of the United Kingdom Male and Female Street-sellers and Hawkers' Union. The ceremony was performed by Mr. Will Crooks, M.P.. who, during the performance of a well-arranged programme of various items, sat in a box with Mrs. Crooks, Mrs. Kline (Woolwich Guardian), Miss Lake, the Mayor of Woolwich, and Councillor Alfred Hall. Others present included Messrs. C. C. Gibson, president of the union; K. Mendez, vice-president; J. F. Jefferson, F. J. Phayer and H. Brown, trustees; F. C. Harding, C. Channing, J. Gilbert, W. Dennard, C. Rumsey, T. W. H. Wright, G. Mansfield, J. Barnett, W. Holmes, H. Arnsby, committee; Mr. F. Wilkesbarre and H. J. Cohen, official organisers; W. Owen and A. Segain, auditors; G. S. Henderson, general secretary; and C. Robinson, assistant secretary.

In addition to the ordinary turns, special items were rendered by Harry Weston (son of a member), Harry Wright (hon. member). Pad-dy Gilbert (hon. member) and Harry Broughton (hon. member), and Ruffle's Bioscope, which showed some excellent pictures of Wollwich Market.

During an interval in the programme, the ceremony of unfurl-ing took place. In the first house it was done by Mr. Crooks, who, with the Mayor and Councillors, occupied seats on the stage. The chair was taken by Mr. Gibson. Prior to the unfurling, the "Banner Song," composed by Mr. F. Robinson, was admirably sung by Mr. Har-ry Broughton, the chorus being rendered by the choir of the union, which was also on the stage.

The chairman, in introducing the member for Woolwich, said they had met for a good purpose. Very nearly twelve months ago the idea came into their heads that they would form a combination for self-protection, and be was glad to say that they had succeeded im-mensely up to the present. The chief idea of the organisation was to defend its members from any unjust attack made upon them in the pursuit of their calling. With regard to the special business in hand, on February 4th they had an entertainment in the Theatre Royal, by kind permission of Mr. Barnard, and by that they realised the sum of £35, with which they had purchased a banner and regalia.

Mr. Crooks, who was most cordially received, said he must first congratulate Woolwich on the possession of such a fine singer as Mr. Broughton, who would do credit to any town. It was extremely kind and generous of him to come amongst them that night. Referring to their organisation, he said that with a man at their lead like the chairman he did not think they need fear suffering any injustice. But the representatives of justice sometimes saw a little more than really happened, said it was well that, should occasion require it, there should be someone ready to explain to the magistrate. While enrolled under that banner they would be able to let people see that, although they had to get their living in the streets, in all weathers, and not always under the best of conditions, they were respectable – and very respectable – people. The shopkeeper, and the shop assistant knew what difficulties they were under. They could tell them of how some people spent half-an-hour in a shop, and then bought a halfpenny worth of pins, while the street seller often had to put up with a lot of people staring at his stall instead of moving on and making room for those who had money to spend. He hoped that they would maintain their dignity and pride for the work they had to do. They had to put up with a deal, he knew, and be tolerant with people who were not very tolerant themselves. He had always found, and he spoke from ripe experience, that men and women were respected in accordance with the measure of respect they had for themselves, and therefore every member must be careful of his or her own dignity, as well as the dignity of the association. He congratulated the chairman and the union, which was equal with any other Trade Union in the country.

The banner, when unfurled, was found to be of blue silk, with a deep border of crimson. It bore the words, "United Kingdom Male and Female Streetsellers and Hawkers' Union – Unity is Strength." The design consisted of a fine representation of the market in Beresford Square, showing the stalls and shops round the Square, surmounted by emblems of fruit and bowers. It was very pretty, and capitally executed.

Mr. Councillor Hall, being called upon, said he must congratulate the streetseller and hawker upon the success they had achieved. Solicitors, doctors, carpenters, engineers and others had their unions. and why not they? He hoped that every success would attend the branch.

Mr. Jefferson moved a vote of thanks to Mr. Crooks and Councillor Hall. When he first took a business he had hut one object – himself and his business. He had had 25 years' experience up and down the country, and he knew the hardships of a streetseller's life. He had always found that the fairer they dealt with the general public, the fairer the public dealt with them. He meant to do all he could for the branch, which had his fullest sympathy.

The vote of thanks being seconded, it was duly carried, and the proceedings concluded.

At the "second house," the proceedings were very similar to those recorded above, excepting that the Mayor of Woolwich (the Rev. L. Jenkins Jones, L.C.C., J.P.) unfurled the banner. He was supported by Councillors Turnbull, jun. and Hall.

The chair was again taken by Mr. Gibson. Mr. Councillor Messent, the ex-Mayor, being unable to attend on amount of being out-of-town.

The Mayor's remarks were very brief. He said it gave him great pleasure to be amongst his fellow citisens. He recognised the necessity on the part of people to combine for the purpose of obtaining the justice which each man was entitled to as a citizen of the Empire or the Borough in which he lived. Labour was dignified. It did not matter whether it was the Prime Minister or the gentleman whom circumstances decreed he should be King, so long as he laboured with dignity. No man need be ashamed to carry on his work, whatever it might be, provided he did it in the proper spirit. No occupation that was legal was degrading. It was rather the people who degraded the occupation. He hoped that those who went out into the streets to sell, or had a stall in the market, would never forget that they were in every way entitled to the same privileges as the greatest citizen in the country.

Mr. Turnbull said he was gratified to be present. He thought that if it was a good thing for those in factories to combine, it was a good thing also for those who sold their goods in the streets and market places to combine also.

Surfessor of Egoism— Introduction
Trevor Blake (2018)

"SURFESSOR OF EGOISM" [sic] is a delightful and informative and previously uncollected work about (and possibly by) Malfew Seklew. This article appeared in the *Manchester Guardian* Number 27,469 (September 25th, 1934) on page 20. Do the initials "M. S." found at the end of the article indicate that Man Without a Soul was writing about himself? Or does the curious misspelling of "Sirfessor" indicate this article is by another?

Hyde Park, where this article "might" have taken place, is the location of Speakers' Corner. Decades after egoist Sirfessor Seklew spoke there, so did egoist S. E. Parker. Columbus Circle is at the intersection of Broadway, 8th Avenue, Central Park South and Central Park West in New York City.

Sirfessor Seklew was not the only one to sniff at the description of sausages as "hot dogs" — this objection is found in the heroic titular character found in *Outbursts of Everett True* (Baltimore: Underworld Amusements 2015).

The article gives a physical description of the Sirfessor entirely complementary to the illustration by Josh Latta in *The Gospel According to Malfew Seklew* (Baltimore: Underworld Amusements 2014). The Sirfessor is described as "Johnsonian," after British essayist Dr. Samuel Johnson (1709 — 1784). The content of his oration is also in harmony with *The Gospel According to Malfew Seklew*, the very pamphlet the Sirfessor is soapboxing here (expanded with additional material and a new introduction in the Underworld Amusements edition).

Sirfessor Seklew (circa 1860s — 1938) drops the names of men he said he knew. Ulysses S. Grant (1822 — 1885) was General of the Union Army and the 18th President of the United States. Mark Twain (1835 — 1910) was an author. William Morris (1834 — 1896) was an artist and socialist. Charles Bradlaugh (1833 — 1891) was a Member of Parliament for Northampton and founded the National Secular Society. Robert Ingersoll (1833 — 1899) was an orator on the subject of agnosticism. Emma Goldman (1869 — 1940) was an anarchist and author. These lives overlapped; what the Sirfessor meant by "know" (exchanged letters? close companions?) is not known. Grant and Twain lived in the State of New York when Sirfessor Seklew did. Bradlaugh and Ingersoll shared the freethought that Sirfessor Seklew did. Warren Starr Van Valkenburgh mentioned Malfew by moniker to Emma Goldman in a July 1932 letter. This author concludes it is not impossible that Sirfessor Seklew was telling the gospel truth.

No supercrat is curtailed by mere chronology, consistency or correctness. The *Manchester Guardian* reports the Sirfessor "never Americanized himself." Malfew Seklew described "himself as an alien, seeing the country the American fashion" when summoned before the Newcastle Bench on charges of obstruction according to the *Shields Daily Gazette* of August 31st, 1901. J. M. Barrie published *When a Man's Single* in 1888 (London: Hodder and Stoughton). The book was published again by the International Book Company of New York circa 1890 — 1899. John Basil Barnhill (better known to readers of *Der Geist* as John Erwin McCall and the editor of *The Eagle and The Serpent*) founded a company also called the International Book Company in Canton, Illinois. And Seklew was a clerk at the Nottingham Journal when Barrie was writing *When a Man's Single*. As Charles Fort said in *Lo!* (New York: C. Kendall 1931): "One measures a circle, beginning anywhere."

The *New York Evening Post* for April 15th, 1930 made mention of one of Seklew's lost works, *Forty Years of Soap-Boxing*. The *New York Times* (February 10th, 1938) reported that when a reporter called on the last residence of Sirfessor Fred M. Wilkes that he was met by "Wilkes' Boswell" who gave his name as "Potter." This article from the *Guardian* gives us the full name William Potter, and shows the two together in 1934 and 1938. Our research department is in swift pursuit of William Potter.

SURFESSOR OF EGOISM
M. S.   (1934)

It might have been Hyde Park, only it happened to be Columbus Circle, beneath the lights of Broadway and an advertisement for chewing-gum. He stood alongside other lesser orators on his own little soap-box, among vendors of "hot dogs" and, hamburgers, peanuts and Coca Cola, with the American flag tightly furled and poking up stiffly beside him like an umbrella in a stand. His warm, comforting accent gave him away as Yorkshire.

He was clearly a man who would stand no nonsense.

"I don't want any half-baked organisms here," he was expostulating. "Half-wits, go away! Anyone nasty-minded, go away! I must have the respectful silence of the people or I shall pack up my duds and walk."

He looked down severely through his rimless spectacles, a small, stoutish man of Johnsonian aspect, with locks of grey hair sprouting beneath a black trilby and a sheaf of papers under one arm. He was trying to remember a name.

"We'll have to let it go," he said reluctantly to his disappointed disciples. "If you can't think about a thing, don't let it distress you. I don't let anything disturb me now."

Then, wiping his brow and tipping his trilby to a rakish angle, he drew himself up for his final peroration.

"To conclude. One law governs all fermentations and combinations. What is that law? Selfishness is the law that governs all life. Every man is composed of trillions of cells, and every cell is an egoist. There's no such thing as society. The only thing on earth is the individual. I am not only a prophet; I am the voice of nature."

"But I'm a part of nature, too," interrupted a man in a straw hat, chewing a cigar and blocking everyone's view.

"You are a depraved part of nature," continued the orator serenely.

"Judged by whose intellect?"

"Nature's intellect."

"He's knocking hell out of that guy, though he don't know it," someone murmured, rejoicing at the retort. "Listen, Professor. Can you tell us how to rejuvenate our youth?" The question was put seriously.

"Surfessor," corrected the Britisher. "Surfessor of the Society of Social Supercrats and Conscious Egoists. Everything on earth is understood if you read our pamphlets. The purpose of life and how to abolish ignorance and poverty from the face of the earth! How mind moulds matter to its own shape! And why? Because I've got a new definition of mind and matter."

"I'm charging you ten cents because I want you to express your selfishness in a social way. I don't sell the paper. I sell the brain-power there. Only for high-class organisms. There's two more. Will you have them or will you not!"

He offered them as if they were the Sibylline prophecies. An admirer pooled ten cents in order that a copy might be given to the unemployed.

"You have socialised your selfishness to the extent of ten cents," commented the philosopher, unable to let slip this example of the conscious egoist. "You have experienced the highest form of psychic satisfaction. This is the demonstration of a man who can give his surplus value away."

Then he pivoted cautiously on his soap-box, hesitating. To the old man the ground seemed far away.

"As I fall on the world, hear it shake," he said, charging his solid little jump with significance.

"Wait to speak to me, young lady? Yes, Yorkshire. I knew everyone in Bradford worth knowing — Edinburgh, Glasgow, Manchester, Leeds — used to pitch in Victoria Square. I was the first soap-box orator to give Nietzsche to the world. *Forty Years a Soap Boxer*, title of my next book!"

"William, are you ready?"

An unobtrusive Boswell emerged, from the crowd.

"This is the famous Mr. Potter," explained the philosopher. "You haven't heard my seven stages of psychic progression. Well, William has reached the fifth stage."

Ignoring traffic signals, the philosopher stepped into Broadway and the traffic drew to a screeching, angry halt.

"The Surfessor is built like a block house," complained William. "He refuses to be disturbed. It's a fact. But I'm more of a nervous temperament."

"I knew General Grant, Mark Twain, William Morris, Bradlaugh,

Ingersoll," continued the Surfessor blandly.

"And don't forget Emma Goldman," prompted Mr. Potter mournfully.

"I was a clerk in the same office as J. M. Barrie — *Nottingham Journal* — when he was writing *When a Man's Single*. I once offered Bernard Shaw a job as editor of the *Malfew Seklew Journal*, but since *Man and Superman* he hasn't done a thing worth a damn, not from our standpoint."

He shook his head as if in Shaw's apostasy all the stupidity of mankind were symbolised.

"There's no man that would disagree with what the Surfessor says if they understood him, but they don't understand him," was William's explanatory note. "He's never Americanised himself."

We neared a restaurant. From the empty ocean of his pocket the Surfessor of Egoism fished out four modest nickels.

"William, go and get us some coffee," he said with a grandiloquent gesture. "And may the blessing of Malfew Seklew, the most high-class organism that ever flew through space, rest upon your alabaster brow."

Seeing his obvious poverty we hesitated.

"I do it just because it's my pleasure, you know," he said gruffly. "Just giving away surplus value."

A New Way to Earn a Living
Malfew Seklew   (1914)

> SIMPOLEONS! Listen! Don't be blisters on the Bosom of Time, but look like Napoleons of Labour by wearing "Sericine" Silk Ties. Something new. Seklew's Sample Shilling Set: 3 Ties, 1 Tie-maker, 1 silver-cased Collar-fastener. 1s. the Lot. Agents wanted. Particulars 1d.— Seklew and Co., 11, Chester-str.t C.-on-M., Manchester.

SIMPOLEONS! Listen! Don't be blisters on the Bosom of Time, but look like Napoleons of Labour by wearing "Sericine" Silk Ties. Something New. Seklew's Sample Shilling Set: 3 Ties, 1 Tie-Maker, 1 silver-cased Collar-fastener. 1s the Lot. Agents wanted. Particulars 1d. – Seklew and Co., 11, Chester-street, C.-on-M., Manchester.– *Daily Herald* March 20th, 21st, 23rd, 24th, 26th, 27th and 28th 1914.

> A NEW WAY to earn a living. New Invention. Just out. Genuine Moneymaker. Samples, 1s. Comrade Barre earned £3 12s. last week. —Particulars from Seklew and Co., 11, Chester-street, Manchester. (C).

A NEW WAY to earn a living. New invention. Just out. Genuine Moneymaker. Samples, 1s. Comrade Barre earned £3 12s. last week. – Particulars from Seklew and Co., 11, Chester-street, Manchester.– *Daily Herald* April 8th, 20th, 21st, 23rd, 29th, 30th; May 2nd, 4th and 5th 1914.

HOUSEWIVES! Washing-day a pleasure not a bore. Use our special 'Scrub-no-more.' 7d secures recipe. – M. SEKLEW & Col., 268, Rutherglen Road, Glasgow.– *Western Chronicle* November 27th; December 4th 1908.

COMRADES! Pocket your own profits. Send 1d. stamp for particulars of our latest quick-selling line to M. Seklew and Co., 11, Chester-street, Oxford road, Manchester.– *Daily Herald* March 14th and 17th 1914.

AGENCY vacant; quick-selling line; easy to carry and small outlay. Samples 7d., from SEKLEW & Co., 11, Chester St., Oxford RJ., Manchester.– *Whistable Times* and *Herne Bay Herald* March 14th, 21st and 28th 1914; *Western Chronicle* April 3rd 1914.

NOVELTIES, New. – Smoker's Cinema, Mystic Photos, Mysterious Postcards, and Living Picture Postcards. Sample lot 6d. Also one Sericine Silk Necktie and Patent Tie-folder. Sample 6. Listen, Sirfessor Wilkesbarre, Jester-Philosopher, author of "The Swiftest Molecule of Mirth that ever Murdered a Microbe of Misery," writes in syllabilious sentence, thusly: "Your Novelties are abso-bally-lutely mar-veel-ious. ["] Resellers investigate. – Seklew and Co. 11, Chester-street, Oxford-road, Manchester. — *Daily Herald* – Tuesday 16 June 1914

Portrait and Biographical Sketch from the *Labor Annual*

Uncredited (1900)

MALFEW SEKLEW,
LIBERTARIAN-SOCIALIST.

Seklew, Malfew, b. Sheffield in '63. Was at *Nott'm Journal* same time as J.M.Barrie; in America 15 year., and worked at almost everything not respectable, including running for Congress. An amusing and lively prophet of the new Egoist-Materialist-Libertarian-Socialist School. Has a striking personality, deep earnestness, and strong character, and is not dead yet.—c/o *Truthseeker*, 36 Villiers-st., Bradford.

THE PERFUMED PIGS OF PARADISE
MALFEW SEKLEW (1903)

Re the ILP Club Room Controversy
To the Editor of the *Bradford Daily Telegraph*

Sir, – Mr. A. T. Sutton knows as much about this affair as a pig knows about the perfumes of paradise. I would suggest that this poor mis-guided human document should cease to exhibit his second-hand thoughts until he has ascertained the truth concerning it. Mr. Sutton not only tramples on the truth, but murders it. He has moral *delirium tremens*, and cannot think clearly while in this condition. The dogma-tism of A. T. S. is pitiable. He seems to be anxious to spread himself, whether right or wrong. When he denies that a member of the Gir-lington ILP Club called at Mr. Gott's residence on the Sunday after-noon previous to the date for the contest, he assassinates the truth and talks through his whiskers. I was present when this committee-man called, and we three went straight away to the meeting, where Mr. Sutton and other great men of this picayune party were biting lumps off the atmosphere in their agony, trying to solve this mighty problem. I trust the day is far distant when these majestic minds will dominate the destinies of the nation. For ineptitude, vacillation, and merciless juggling with the truth they are – well, let the public judge.
Yours, etc.
MALFEW SEKLEW
Bradford, Feb 28.

STARS IN THE TALKING MARATHON
UNCREDITED *(1924)*

Sirfessor Wilkesbarre stand before his tent on January 2nd 1929, in the *Vidette-Messenger* of Porter County. The caption to this image reads:

Speaking of Marathons, here's a speaking marathon, staged in New York by Milton Crandall, who invented the dance marathon. The contestant who talks the most during the 5-day gab-fest wins the $1,000 prize. In the rear are seen Madame Anet Barrie, 51, who used to be on the stage and is kept busy telling about it now, and F. M. Wilkesbarre, 65, whom you mustn't interrupt while he discourses on "superology" of which he is the "Lord of Interpretation." In the foreground are D. F. O'Brien. 65, who speaks on his past life as "king of the hoboes," and Mrs. Jean Cabell O'Neill, 56, who guarantees to talk on any subject, any time, any place and forever!

The *New York Daily News* of December 28th, 1928 ran a piece about the contest. While the photo included does not feature the Sirfessor, it does mention him in the article. Seklew dropped out after the second day, but he was such a stand out character he is mentioned in much of the coverage of the event.

The caption for the above photo from the *New York Daily News* reads:

At the talking marathom. L. to r.: Capt. Smoke, Chief Hawk, Betty Wilson, Andrea Di Gierco, Mme. Anet Barrie, Nurse Grossman.

VICTOR GRAYSON, M. P.— INTRODUCTION
TREVOR BLAKE (2018)

Victor Grayson, M. P. / A Rhapsody on a Reality is known to exist in a single copy. *Der Geist* reprints this work for the first time since its initial publication circa 1909.

Victor Grayson includes an advertisement for the Society of Social Aristocrats and Conscious Egoists. Malfew Seklew is listed as President. We know of the good Sirfessor not only from this Epistle but from the very *Gospel According to Malfew Seklew*. Spencella Maljean is listed as the Secretary. The "Questions of the Hour" section of *Victor Grayson* is the only known example of her writing. A letter from "T. T." of Winnipeg, Canada in *The Day Book* Volume 5 Number 128 (February 25th, 1916) mentions "the greatest of all women of Scottish birth, Spencella Maljean." The *Gospel According to Malfew Seklew* was published by Spencella and Winsex. *Victor Grayson*, a letter in *Day Book* and a publisher's name are the sum total of Spencella Maljean in print. But of the Society's Treasurer, Wilson Canochan, nothing at all is known.

Malfew Seklew was not the only man to offer left-handed compliments to the socialist Victor Grayson. In the pages of *Pravda* (Number 109, May 14th, 1913), one V. Lenin described Grayson as "a very fiery socialist, but one not strong in principles and given to phrase-mongering." Grayson ran a parallel track to Dora Marsden. Grayson was elected as a Member of Parliament in Coln, near Dora's birthplace, both of them worked at Manchester College, both (for a time) advocated votes for women, and both appeared in the pages of *The New Age* magazine. Victor Grayson vanished in September 1920.

Victor Grayson refers to many public figures of the early 1900s. Andrew Scott Gibson is described as "a populist muck-raking orator" from Glasgow in *Dictionary of Labour Biography* Volume XIV by Gildart & Howell (London: Palgrave Macmillan 2018). A "Cheap Jack" is a peddler or a coster. John Burns (1858 — 1943) was a socialist then labor MP who resigned from politics at the beginning of World War One. Robert Blatchford (1851 — 1943) was a socialist, an atheist and an opponent of eugenics. Maxim Gorki (1868 — 1936) was an author whose support for the early Soviet Union was rewarded by Lenin with exile. Bart Kennedy (1861 — 1930) was a novelist. The Manchester School of Economists or Manchester Liberalism advocated free trade and a free press.

Historic and literary references are also found in *Victor Grayson*. Lochinvar appears in "Marmion" (1808) by Scottish poet Sir Walter Scott (1771 — 1832). John Ball (1338 — 1381) was a priest and a leader in the Peasants' Revolt of 1381. "To a Skylark" (1820) by Percy Bysshe Shelley (1792 — 1822) includes: "We look before and after / And pine for what is not / Our sincerest laughter / With some pain is fraught / Our sweetest songs are those that tell of saddest thought." *A Young Man in a Hurry* is a 1904 collection of short stories by Robert W. Chambers (1865 — 1933), author of *The King in Yellow*. *A Window in Thrums* is a 1897 novel by J. M. Barrie (1860 — 1937). Thrums is a fictional town based on the author's memory of his childhood in Kirriemuir, but after Barrie achieved fame for his *Peter Pan* books a real Thrums was founded. Ancoat is an area of Manchester. "To be or not to be" and "all the world is a stage" are paraphrased quotes from the plays of William Shakespeare (1564 — 1616). Alfred, Lord Tennyson (1809 — 1892) was Poet Laureate of Great Britain and Ireland. Ecclesiastes 9:11 reads: "I saw that the race is not to the swift, nor the battle to the strong, nor bread to the wise, nor riches to men of understanding, nor favor to men of skill; but time and chance happen to them all."

There are many figures and quotes referenced in *Victor Grayson* that are also referenced in *Might is Right* by Ragnar Redbeard. Oliver Cromwell (1599 — 1658) was the Lord Protector of the Commonwealth of England. Henrik Ibsen (1828 — 1906) was a playwright. The Torah, the Bible and the Quran all describe Gehenna as the destination for wicked souls after death. Robinson Crusoe is a character in a 1719 novel by Daniel Defoe (1660 -1731). Robin Hood was a fictional guerrilla first mentioned in the late Fourteenth Century, known for "robbing from the rich and giving to the poor." The phrase "*Et in terra pax*" or "Peace on earth," is a quotation from Luke 2:14. Each of these appears in both texts. Bart Kennedy (1861 — 1930) was a novelist mentioned by Seklew in *Victor Grayson*. *The Sayings of Ragnar Redbeard* (Chicago: House of Gowrie 1927) writes of Kennedy's *Gospel of Physical Courage*: "This is a ripping good pamphlet on the whole, by a man who can write better than Jack London." Where

Spencella writes "the more intellectual the animal, the more sterile it tends to become," Redbeard writes: "As the Old Man of the Mountains trained his fanatical assassins and sent them forth to slay, so civilization trains its fiendling intellectuals and sends them forth to assassinate man's nature. They are the murderers of manliness, the regicides of thought, the annihilators of heroism." Ragnar Redbeard and Malfew Seklew had met in the pages of *The Eagle and The Serpent* in years prior to the publication of *Victor Grayson*. I suggest the other "learned gentleman" in *Victor Grayson* is Ragnar Redbeard.

Victor Grayson promotional postcard circa 1909.

Victor Grayson, M. P. /
A Rhapsody on a Reality
Malfew Seklew, Spencella Maljean (1909)

Albert Victor Grayson, the victorious Revolutionist of Colne Valley, is the young Lochinvar of the North-West of England who broke into the House of Commons amid the hurrahs and hosannas of one million jubilant Socialists.

On his alabaster brow he wears a nibus of victory decorated with the motto: — "For Socialism and Colne Valley."

He is the first avowed Socialist in England to enter the Portals of the House of Privilege, Piffle, and Plunder; and the first Herald of Socialism in Parliament to blow the Bugle of Alarm, to sound the Clarion of Class-concsiousness, or to tickle the Tocsin of Talkology.

He is a clean shaven, smooth haired, strenuous young man of slim build; a man, who has lived and can [talk]. Optimistic Soothsayer that he is, he can declaim with the fluency of a Scott Gibson, the effectiveness of a Cheap Jack, the Enthusiasm of a John Ball, the audacity of a John Burns, the mental outlook of a Robert Blatchford, and the intentions of a Cromwell.

He is the intellectual Swashbuckler of Socialism ready to perish for his principles and party — or accept a portfolio in the Cabinet — which he undoubtedly deserves — if he gets the chance.

A Humanitarian, who eats meat — although a dear friend of an eminent, virtuous vegetarian — he is the protégé of Robert Blatchford, who has given him a fillip that fills him with confidence enough to defeat his foes, should they ever meet him at Philippi.

Once a tramp — like Maxim Gorki, Bart Kennedy, Malfew Seklew and other rebels against a system of unequal opportunity — he became a Socialist Mob Orator; then a Journalist; and now is the Leader of a new Political Party in Parliament, composed of — Himself for, as Ibsen says "the strongest man is he who best stands alone" — till disciples gather round.

As the Robinson Crusoe of the Political Socialist Crusaders, he is proud of his own Ego — and "The Clarion" and the Proletariat are proud of him. Developer of his own individuality and struggling to be the master of his own environment, he stands erect, single handed, unmarried, and — like a stalwart — with a broken bottle in one hand, he pours forth a broadside of mental bullets into the brainpans of his Antagonists.

But he is likewise a "two handed" Orator, for he takes hold of his subject with both hands and manipulates, with all his magic, the mainspring of his opponent's argument — when the spirit moves him.

He is certainly not of Tallyrand's opinion that language was given to man to enable him to conceal his thoughts, for sometimes he can talk eloquently — without thought — when struggling in the slough of sentiment.

He has not yet become subdued with sorrow or stagnation of sensation, and, when on the platforms, thrills his auditors with sympathetic vibrations, and vitalises them with the vigor of his perorations. Albeit, even in his most hilarious mood, there is an undertone of sadness. The spirit of sorrow remains with him, as if in verification of that beautiful phrase: -

"Our sweet songs are those that tell of saddest Thought."

He is a young man in a hurry (sometimes) to save the world before he dies, and he does not mind being turned upside down himself occasionally, so long as he may have a chance of turning the world right side up.

His present aim is "to find work for the unemployed, food for the hungry, and clothes for the naked"; and, after that, to lay the foundation stone of a University of Humanity, where they can be taught how to "make the conquest of the intellectual and artistic world," and thus establish "the most beautiful edifice which has ever been constructed" — the Utopia of the Idealist and Sobbist.

He is a Messenger of Mercy from Manchester with an Evangel, which will change the constitution from Chaos to Concord, and from Misery to Mirth. He is working day and night to rescue the Masses from Gehenna, and to rid "Society" of the Pharisee and Parasite.

Led by this Missionary from Manchester, the Masses march through a Monsoon of Misery to the Milennium — the Mecca of the Mob — regardless of the Manchester School of Economists and the *laissez-faire* principle.

He works hard for Humanity's sake, perhaps unmindful that it is the customary fate of New Truths to begin as heresies and end as superstitions.

He is possessed with a desire to live to see the Spirit of a New Age touch and change the ideals of the poor and rouse them into a recognition of their true worth and power — and yet there are some who say that he wishes to rob the rich to help the poor — as did Robin Hood of old.

In his leisure moments, he often takes a walk in the Realm of Thought to feel the pulse of an impulse of the people and to vivisect the Vice of Virtue and the Virtue of Victory.

Anon he sits at a window—not in Thrums—but in Ancoat's Slums, and soliloquizes as he sips his tea from the Saucer of sorrow — and ruminates over the Romance of a Victorious Rebel—Himself.

"All the World is a stage," and men and women (and politicians) are merely players. Some play many parts; Grayson has one that suits him — that of a Politician with a Proposal, a Purpose, and a Panacea. His Proposal has created a panic among the opponents of Socialism, who believe it would create a pandemic and his Panacea a Pandemonium, while Grayson himself believes that his Panacea will bring "Peace on earth, good will towards men." As Tennyson says:— "It is the motive, the great purpose, that consecrates life," and in the Zenith of his Fortitude—Grayson has dedicated his life to the Emancipation of the Working Classes.

Great is Victor Grayson of the Socialists — among Socialists!

This Rhapsody is now ruptured — by silence.

Questions of the Hour. No. 1. Should Ignorance be disturbed?
by Spencella Maljean

"To be or not to be—that is the question; whether it is better for Humanity that woman should remain ignorant, and become 'unsexed' —or, gaining intellect—become sterile and hasten to extermination of His Nobility—Man?"

This burning question has suddenly flashed across the threshold of my brain, and clamors tumultuously for a satisfactory reply.

The redoutable Victor Grayson, with whom you will now be quaintly acquainted—according to the Epistle of Malfew Seklew— tells us, that woman is becoming "unsexed" through working in Factories—and overworking her body at the expense of her brain.

Another equally learned gentleman (if not more so) tells us with the gravity of Science, that the more intellectual the animal, the more sterile it tends to become — overworking the brain at the expense of the body.

Coupling these ideas together, we deduce the melancholy, albeit cheering, conclusion that Humanity is burning the candle at both ends, and that it is only the great mass of middle-class matter which is saving us from total extinction.

Is it wise, then, to interfere in any way with this centre of our civilization — the equidistant, mediocre, middle class? Are we not in so doing, rashly rushing into the arms of death? Were it not the wiser way to let nature do her own work—as far as she can 'midst such civilised saints?

Or is it, perchance, nobler to die of Intellectual Tremens than of Factories?

"The race is to the strong," and it may interest those of us who are philosophic to watch the encroachments of ignorance and intellect upon the Impregnable Rock of Massive Mediocrity, and imagine ourselves "in at the death."

Vol. III.—No. 18.   OAKLAND, CAL., AUGUST 28, 1896.   Price, Five Cents.

Egoism

Fortnightly, 50 cents a Year.

EQUITY PUBLISHING COMPANY,

Oakland, California.

Postoffice Box 366.

Entered at Oakland, Cal., as Mail Matter of the Second Class.

Pointers.

The gold monopolists of the East are no more anxious for partners in their pot than the proposed silver monopolists of the West are going to be for universal partnership of the same kind when their game is potted. The railroads

York "Liberty" says Mr. Fulton is not quite finished in economics and will have like Hugh O. Pentecost to learn in public. Now I take Mr. Tucker's word on almost any point except the cessation of property rights in human clam culture, and am willing to jump into Mr. Fulton wherever I think I can show off to advantage. Meanwhile I welcome him to sharing the annoyance and expense of educating the woolly Philistine in my political faith. If the reform business were a money-making one in which co‑‑‑‑‑ut profits, it would be different, but as it ‑‑‑‑‑‑ to see an Anarchistic paper at every count‑‑‑ the s‑‑‑. This of course, provided most of th‑‑‑‑s were plumbliners, for Anarchism is in most da‑‑‑‑m its worst enemy, its friends. The subscript‑‑‑‑‑‑e of Thought" is a dollar a year. Of ‑‑‑‑‑‑‑s will pay no more attention to thi‑‑‑o any ‑‑‑‑ her

GEORGIA AND HENRY REPLOGLE / *EGOISM*

Egoism was the first English-language egoist journal, published by individualist anarchists Georgia and Henry Replogle beginning in 1890. *Egoism* is notable for first serializing Walker's book *The Philosophy of Egoism*. It also contained writings by and about the anarchist and individualist discussions of the day. While Walker's book would later be reprinted as a single volume in 1905, the journal became scarce and is nearly impossible to access until the publication of *Egoism: The First Two Volumes 1890-1892* (Baltimore: Union of Egoists, 2017).

Egoism Vol. II, No. 18, August 19th, 1896. Care of Labadie Collection.

ARTICLES IN THIS SECTION

Egoism's Purpose and Whyfore
Georgia and Henry Replogle (1897)

Egoism's purpose is to make the Ego — the I, master, rather than the slave of his environment. To impel him to the self-entertaining sufficiency for his psychological cravings which places their gratification ever farther from the mercy of other's whims. To quicken him into full understanding and appreciation of his biological prerogatives, and to press him to their prompt assertion and defense. And, finally, to gain general recognition for a standard of Ethics and Social Polity based on a logical extension of biological order into the social realm.

Such biological order becomes protrudingly obvious when we analyze the physical basis of psychical projection, and note that an Ego is the sum total of consciousness manifested by an organism physiologically separate from the others of any species; that this consciousness is impossible without setting everything second to itself; that hence for the Ego to contemplate ultimate reference to anything but its own satisfaction must be as impossible as it is for consciousness to exist without positing itself prior to the objects it is conscious of; that therefore Self-Interest is psychologically as legitimate as physiological separation is imperative by the organic processes that bring it into existence, and that each one lives, or suicides, exactly in the degree that he conforms to this absolute order of his being.

Society is nothing other than an aggregation of such Egos. One of these can be nothing to another except as he detracts from or adds to that other's happiness. On this is based the concept of the social compromise known as justice. The resistance of each individual determines what is expedient as such compromise, and as that resistance is necessarily approximatively equal, such approximative equality is the only enduring term of social compact.

It follows, then, that the basic principle of consistent Social Polity is not a relation of the Majority with the Individual or of the Individual with the Majority as practiced in Majority Rule, but of Individual with Individual, as of nation with nation in international relations. This, therefore, leaves rational defense for neither Minority dictation nor Majority coercion, but requires in all matters political, a strict conformity to the equal freedom terms of Individual Autonomy. And the very nature of this Imperial Democracy demands that the regulations of the social compromise be enforced by the citizens *en masse*, else all of the imperial divisions of social prerogative would not be sharing in the dispatch of their function and in the responsibility for its manner. Such a court function could with requisite representation be most expeditiously administered by jury trial in its original form, which empowered a jury chosen by lot from the mass of citizens, to judge the fitness of the law as well as the sufficiency of evidence. Thus the people could in the light of Equal Freedom dispose of each case of whatsoever kind upon its own merits, without impediment from the inflexibility of statute law, and without danger from either the bias or corruptibility of a court constituted in a single individual known as the wielder of such power before the day of trial. This system of political administration would confine political authority to its legitimate function, that of restraining invasion, and would be real, not "government of the people by the people," but defense of the people by the people. It would annihilate political meddling, by destroying it as an industry from which men may gain an easy livelihood, and would inaugurate the era of real sovereignty — Liberty with Responsibility.

Ethically, the Egoist knows no motive of anybody's except the direct or ultimate satisfaction of the Ego, and recognizes no "duty" to anything nor anybody by anybody. Thus conceding duty to no one and exacting it from no one, he openly posits a basis for action about which there can be no misunderstanding and which will place every person squarely on the merit of his probable interests, divested of the opportunity to deceive through other pretension, as under the dominance of Altruistic idealism.

He may do apparently Altruistic conduct to secure self-satisfactions that are to be had in no cheaper way and still be working Egoistically, for all satisfaction is Egoistic. Egoistic conduct therefore makes for general happiness, for just as the Egos are happiest happiness is general.

This is the Egoistic ideal as against that of the rationally impossible Altruist, who, has but one consistent course of conduct, and that is to avoid every selfish attribute. He must work constantly for other than self; he must not even choose for whom he works, for there is choice, self-coming in again; he must not even choose to be Altrurian, for choice is selfism; he must be an idiot.

Politically, the consistent Egoist can sanction no government of man by man save in the sense of defense — defense of that equal liberty which is the logical and necessary compromise of Egoic equal resistance as manifested both by personal capacity to resist and by the sympathy of the onlooker. Necessity thus positing the only needful law there is no use for enactment, and recognizing no political superior there is no political function which he cannot perform or which he could afford to delegate. He is, in short, an Anarchist — an Egoistic Anarchist, and the literature of Egoistic Anarchism alone can answer the questions that acquaint with the only invulnerable political philosophy.

Minus the Communist
Georgia Replogle   *(1897)*

Box 366
Oakland Calif.
Feb 4 '97

M. Nettlau,
Dear Sir:
Your card does not state whether you mean *Egoisms* commecing with Vol. 1, but I suppose you do. We can no longer supply a complete set of Vol. 1, but can give you Vol. 2 and up to No. 20, on Vol. 3. We can send you some numbers of Vol. 1, but Nos. 1, 8, & 7 of that Vol. have been out for some time. However, if you desire, we will send you Vols. 2 & 3, (finishing the present Vol. (3) as fast as they are published) and all the Nos. we have of Vol. 1 and call it two Vols. The price is the same as the regular subscription, 50¢ per year. The postage, I guess, about 15¢, making in all $1.30.

    We could make no use of the Anarchist-Communist literature, as our patrons are minus the communist.

Truly Yours,
Georgia Replogle
for "Egoism."

Pardon the delay, which was due to sickness.

G.

Envelope of 1897 letter from Georgia Replogle,
editor of *Egoism*, to Max Nettlau, anarchist historian.

Box 366,
Oakland, Calif.
M. Nettlou,   Feby. 4 '92.
    Dear Sir:
        Your card does
not state whether you mean.
Egoisms commencing with
vol. 1, but I suppose you
do. We can no long supply
a complete set of vol. 1, but
can give you vol. 2 and up
to no. 20, on vol. 3. We can
send you some numbers
of vol. 1, but nos. 1, 8, & 7 of that
vol. have been out for some
time. However, if you desire,
we will send you vols. 2 & 3,
(finishing the present vol. (3) as fast

First page of letter from Georgia Replogle to Max Nettlau.

2

as they are published)
and all the nos. we have
of vol 1 and call it two
vols. The price is the same
as the regular subscription,
50¢ per year. The postage,
I guess, about 15 ₵, mak-
ing in all $1.15).

We could make no use of
the Anarchist-Communist-
literature, as our patrons
are minus the communist.

Truly yours,
Georgia Replogle.
for "Egoism."

Pardon the delay, which
was due to sickness.

G.

Second page of letter from Georgia Replogle to Max Nettlau.

The "Selfish" Bauble
Henry P. Replogle   (1897)

Outside of posited plumb-line Anarchism and its venereal corollaries, we get no paper in exchange that does not propose saving society by some political magic, except *Progressive Thought*, of Olathe, Kansas, an official organ of the Labor Exchange. But it too has its besetting sin, in the shape of vociferous harp on selfishness, and of course the implied injunction to goodness, without conspicuous emphasis on bald justice and tempting expediency. If selfishness in any sense except that of inexpediency be a bad or unnecessary thing why does not *Progressive Thought* itself dispense with the practice of it as a consistent pose from which to chide the paper's adversaries. If the editors are altogether unselfish why are they concerned about the greed and selfishness of others, or indeed, about anything. If some men wield the power to extort others' production and service and can roll in voluptuous luxury while these others suffer and even die from need of that which they have themselves produced, the first cannot do so to the discomfiture of genuine unselfishness; that lauded and prated and canted attribute could not be selfish enough to begrudge anything to anybody, or even to bewail the fate of the exploited, for that would be choosing — thrusting in self and self's preference decidedly contrary to that good unselfish interposition which belongs alone to dead people.

Now if in this view of it, the *Progressive Thought* people point out that selfishness is in this sense unescapable and necessary, but that there is still a difference between themselves, who struggle for equality of conditions, and those wealthy and powerful who struggle to grasp more and more wealth and power, which difference entitles their conduct to classification as comparative unselfishness; if this be the contention, then I point out that the *Progressive Thought* people do not happen to be wealthy and powerful and haunted by that dread of dependence and comparative insignificance which equality of conditions would impose upon them if they were the wealthy on one side of the line as against the oppressed on the other side or they might see how it is the selfishness of the poorer that seeks equality of conditions for the advantage over worse ones, accounting for much of that equality credit, and thus how the poorer's side of the line makes their choice of choice in the selfish sense, look quite as culpable as the other. It is dread of greater disadvantage and desire for at least equal advantage with their competitors that actuates the rich to grasp; and it is dread of greater disadvantage, and desire for equal advantage with our competitors of which the rich are the greatest, that actuates us who struggle for equal conditions. And, indeed, we go them one better in intensity of selfishness; their selfishness is satisfied with goods, but we not only fight for material conditions each the equal of the best, but besides are satisfied with nothing less than credit in the fight which compels the highest approval of mankind. We insist on the convenience of goods for ourselves and all that can be wrung from the broadest ethics, while they content themselves with goods and its cheap distinction alone. We are not satisfied as they are with possession-pride and material comfort for ourselves, but must have the psychological comfort of having all we look upon between others pander to our choice. So it happens that selfishness is not only the rational motive for conduct, but the most social for the community as a whole. It is only in its blind inexpediency that it can be objectionable, and certainly nothing could be a more striking example of such blindness than the crude manifestation of desiring others to be unselfish or the desire to be so considered ourselves.

Then it turns out that selfishness is the basic principle of human action, of justice as well as of injustice; that justice is the competition of individual selfishness supplemented by intelligence. Hence there is in this line nothing to urge except intelligence, and nothing to chide except inexpediency. We can consistently appeal only to the interests of the oppressed by showing them where and how they are beaten, and to the interests of the oppressors by indicating why it won't pay them to continue. This then leaves the epithet "selfish" either a remissness of analysis to be corrected or a demagogic appeal to indiscriminating crudity, to be despised by just people.

J. WM. LLOYD

John William Lloyd (1857 — 1940) was an individualist anarchist poet and author. Lloyd founded *The Free Comrade*, a magazine edited by Clarence Lee Swartz published between 1900 and 1902. *The Free Comrade* championed anarchism, free love, Whitman ("Our American Shakespeare, and greater than he") and Edward Carpenter ("The greatest man of modern England"). Lloyd wrote two utopian novels, *The Natural Man / A Romance of the Golden Age* (Newark: Benedict Prieth 1902) and *The Dwellers in Vale Sunrise / How They Got Together and Lived Happy Ever After, a Sequel to 'The Natural Man,' Being an Account of the Tribes of Him* (Westwood: Ariel Press 1904).

 The Free Comrade resumed publication in a new series from 1910 to 1912. Lloyd now co-edited it with his friend Leonard D. Abbott, who financed its publication. Between the end of the original series and the beginning of the new, Lloyd had stopped considering himself ananarchist, instead joining the Socialist Party. He wrote: "I am still anarchistic in the essential sense... the great need of Socialism is a stronger infusion of Anarchism... " Meanwhile his friend Abbott had moved from socialism towards anarchism. They offered the new series "as an advocate of the juncture of the Anarchist and Socialist forces."

 Lloyd wrote hundreds of poems, many of which appeared in anarchist periodicals. He was published in Benjamin Tucker's *Liberty*; in Moses Harman's anarchist and free love journal *Lucifer the Light Bearer*; the anarchist and sex-radical newspaper *Fair Play* and others.

Photograph of J. Wm. Lloyd. Care of Labadie Collection.

ARTICLES IN THIS SECTION

First published in *Egoism* Volume 4, Number 1 (September 1897).

This is a transcription of original source material from John William Lloyd. Lloyd was a frequent contributor to Benjamin Tucker's individual anarchist periodical *Liberty* (1881) through most of its lifespan. The following essay "Anarchist Socialism" by Lloyd is undated but it seems to be have been written in the 1920s or '30s. The piece is unedited (by me) except for the deletion of passages with material that would confuse the reader: for example, the mention of Lloyd's obscure acquaintances. The punctuation and grammar is sometimes antiquated and remains so due to my reluctance to edit the work of someone deceased. Despite the word "Socialism" in its title, the essay should be of interest to libertarians. First, it includes a retrospective of Lloyd's own experiences with the 19th Century Anarchist movement, including memories of Tucker and commentary on luminaries such as Josiah Warren. Second, Lloyd was the author of several works, mostly of poetry, that were heavily promoted by *Liberty*; they included "The Anarchists' March," "The Dwellers in Vale Sunrise," and "The Red Heart in a White World." To the extent there is a poet laureate of individualist anarchism, it is surely John William Lloyd. Third, the term "socialism" as used by the 19th Century individualist radicals differed in meaning as dramatically as the word "liberal" today differs from its 18th Century usage. As used by Lloyd and his contemporaries, socialism *per se* — as opposed to State Socialism — did not negate private property or the primacy of the individual but referred more to voluntary, co-operative ventures through which a just society could be achieved. Thus, many of the voluntary communities of early libertarianism could be viewed through either a socialist or individualist lens. To the extent that individualist anarchists who sometimes used the label "socialist" had a point of overlap with collectivist-socialists, it is: they agreed with the labor theory of value. Since individualist anarchists also insisted on the primacy of contract, however, their position devolved to the statement: interest and rent are invalid practices, nevertheless everyone has the right to make a foolish contract, and no third party has the right to interfere. – Wendy McElroy (wendymcelroy.com)

PERSONALLY ACQUAINTED

J. WM. LLOYD   (1897)

A man climbed up a mountain steep,
And far and near his eyeballs peep:
"O what seek you, my friend to find?"
"To find myself, ere I grow blind."

A man went through a forest far,
He dug each root, he watched each star:—
"What seek you, man, in these to find?"
"To find myself, or I grow blind."

A man went o'er a pathless plain
His brain had joy, his feet had pain:—
"If you had luck, what would you find?"
"Who finds himself cannot be blind."

A man sat in the sun and thought;
His every whim his swift hands wrought:—
"What is it then, at last, you find?"
"I find myself, and am not blind."

ANARCHIST SOCIALISM
J. WM. LLOYD   (CIRCA 1917)

As many of you, my comrades, may know me only as a Socialist, and
may doubt my qualifications to explain Anarchism, I will say that for
some 20 years or more I was a professed and active Anarchist, a constant contributor to Anarchist periodicals, and the personal friend
and correspondent of many of the Anarchist leaders of the time. In
1884, when I first publicly announced myself a philosophical Anarchist, *Liberty* was the leading Anarchist paper in the United States
and certainly the ablest one in the world and I became a steady contributor to its columns and the close friend of its editor and owner,
Benj. R. Tucker. Mr. Tucker now lives in Europe, but his wife was
one of the most intimate friends of my family and his only child is
named Oriole, after my daughter. At one time I was the literary editor of *Liberty*. At another I myself edited an Anarchist periodical, *The
Free Comrade*, which was suspended for a while, and then revived for
a short time by Leonard Abbott and myself, as an advocate of the
juncture of the Anarchist and Socialist forces. I also wrote and published an Anarchist booklet, *The Red Heart in a White World* [1898],
and became the leader of an Anarchist group, which was known as
"The Comradeship of Free Socialists," and at one time had quite a
membership, scattered all over the world. My books, *The Natural Man*
[1902] and *Vale Sunrise* [1904], were Anarchistic. During these years,
though I avoided the platform, I was almost constantly engaged in
debate, defending and explaining the philosophy of Anarchism thru
the press. I even wrote an "Anarchist's March," [1888] which was set
to music. I mention all this simply to show you that when I speak of
Anarchism, I am somewhat prepared to explain it and do it justice.
First, then, what is Anarchism? It is logical human liberty. It is the
ideal of human life without a master. Tucker defined it as "Equal Liberty." Another definition is, "Do as you please at your own expense";
another, "Mind your own business and let your neighbor's alone." The
name was first used and applied by Pierre J. Proudhon, the French
philosopher, who derived it from the Greek *an*, privitive, and *archos*,
ruler, meaning life without a ruler or government. On this basis the
Anarchist founds a whole system of ethics and politics. He identifies
crime and government as the same in logical essence, for both are

impositions of one man's will on another without his consent. All Anarchists say that liberty and Anarchism are synonyms.

It was a common charge a few years ago, and probably still is, that Anarchism is an imported foreign product and un-American. On the contrary, Anarchism originated in the United States before the rest of the world had it, and is a logical consequence of fundamental American principles; also many prominent Americans have been Anarchists.

Thomas Jefferson, the author of the Declaration of Independence, was so nearly an Anarchist that he uttered the famous aphorism, "The best government is that which governs the least." The Declaration is so nearly an Anarchist document that there is probably not an Anarchist in the world, except the few Nietzscheans, who would reject its fundamental logic. For example: That all men are equal in rights to life, liberty and pursuit of happiness; That governments derive their just powers from the consent of the governed; That whenever any government becomes destructive to the above rights, it is the right and duty of those who have formed it, the people, to take whatever measures may be necessary to secure their own safety and happiness, even to its complete abolition. In other words, the logic of the Declaration is that the individual is sovereign and supreme where he has his true rights, and the government only his tool, which he has made and has a right, therefore, to unmake at his pleasure.

"Individual Sovereignty" was one of the fundamental American watchwords and the whole of Anarchism is logically included in it. So too, all Anarchism is logically contained in the doctrine that governments derive their just powers from the consent of the governed. No Anarchist has any logical objection to a government to which all its members consent; only he carries the logic one step further and says that if the individual withdraws his consent, in that moment the just power of the government over him ceases. So too, all Anarchism is logically contained in the statement that the right of every man to life, liberty and the pursuit of happiness, in his own inoffensive way, is rightfully inalienable. Therefore the American principles are profoundly Anarchistic and the logic of Anarchism is absolutely American.

But the matter was not left simply to logic and doctrinaire deductions. Josiah Warren, direct descendant of that famous General Warren who fell at Bunker Hill, was the real founder of Anarchism and the first Anarchist author. In his work *True Civilization*, published, I believe in the thirties [1830s], he took the American principle of Individual Sovereignty and worked it out to its logical ultimates, making the first clear and definite presentation of Anarchist principles the world had ever seen. He also established the first Anarchist group at his colony of "Modern Times" on Long Island. However he did not use the word "Anarchism," which had not then been adopted. At that time many prominent Americans accepted these ideas, either wholly or in part. Ralph Waldo Emerson was the most shining example. His writings are full of Anarchist statements of great force, much quoted by Anarchists to this day. His friend, Henry David Thoreau, was a scarcely less illustrious and more militant Anarchist. He went to jail rather than pay a poll-tax to a government that supported slavery. When Emerson heard of it and came to pay his tax to get him out, he said to Thoreau, in his cell, "What Henry, you here!" and Thoreau sarcastically replied, with his quaint Yankee humor, "What, Waldo, and you not here!", implying that to be consistent Emerson would have done the same. And a New England woman, who knew him, told me two summers ago, that his townspeople actually never afterwards asked him to pay a tax. Most of the New England Transcendentalists were more or less Anarchist and so were all Abolitionists, some of whom were radically so, particularly William Lloyd Garrison and Stephen Pearl Andrews. It is noteworthy that the Civil War was more of less avowedly fought over two Anarchist principles, wrested from their context. Thus the North, so far as intentionally Abolitionist, was fighting for the restoration of individuality to the black man, and the South was fighting for the Anarchist principle of Free Secession from an undesired Union.

Warren's most brilliant and influential disciple was Benj. R. Tucker, a man of old New England stock. He was at one time city editor of the *Boston Globe*. As a translator of French books, he translated some of the most important of Proudhon's works and adopted Proudhon's name, Anarchism, for the philosophy. Proudhon had developed his Anarchism separately, with no knowledge of Warren but probably derived it from the logic of the French Revolutionary slogan of "Liberty, Equality and Fraternity," which perhaps the French had largely derived from the principles of the American Revolution with its Declaration of Independence. At any rate its logic was identical. But somewhere near this time, also independently, a Russian form of Anarchism was originated by Bakounine.

Now developed the first split in the Anarchist movement, which since then has broken up fundamentally into many sects and schools. Warren and Proudhon were intensely individualistic, and Proudhon and Tucker especially detested and fought communism, while the Russians made communism their main principle. Bakounine, Kropotkin, and Emma Goldman, all Russians, have been the great leaders of Communistic-Anarchism, which now has largely outgrown the Individualistic-Anarchistic division in numbers and political importance.

Another split grew up over the question of violence. The Individualist-Anarchists have always stood for an intellectual propaganda and for passive resistance, reserving violence only as a weapon of last and desperate resort.

The Russians have largely advocated, encouraged and winked at terrorism as a means of revolution — "propaganda by deed" they called it. A small group of Americans and foreigners combined, in Chicago, at one time and adopted the Russian communistic and terroristic principles, leading to the calamitous "Haymarket Riot," and the hanging of several of their leaders. Among these was Samuel Parsons, also an American of Revolutionary ancestry. On the other hand, among the Russians, Tolstoy developed an entirely new variant of Anarchism — a Christian and non-resistant form, but still communistic. He declared all violence, even in self-defense, a violation of liberty; even to defend liberty, it was a violation of liberty.

Now another split came among the individualists. These had largely adopted the philosophy of Egoism of the German, Max Stirner, who declared all human life was moved simply by self-interest. Still the Americans did not think this conflicted with their principle of equal liberty, which they declared an enlightened egoism would make every man maintain for his own benefit. But Stirner's most brilliant disciple was the German, Nietzsche, who declared that the law of Nature was that might was right, and that the true Anarchist was the individual who cared consciously only for himself and exploited the world to feed his own individuality – who pleased himself and had no law or limit but his own powers. Thru his brilliant and paradoxical genius, Nietzsche exerted a tremendously active influence in the German universities and over the dominating spirits of the world. Theodore Roosevelt is commonly considered among his disciples. So is the German Kaiser and the whole military caste of Germany, and the initiation of the present war is often laid to his door. Napoleon and John Pierpont Morgan could have called themselves Nietzschean Anarchists; or any other utterly unscrupulous exploiter and tyrant might have taken the name.

There was also a small American school whose watchword was "Do as you please and take the consequences!", which they said contained all of Anarchism.

So now Anarchism, today, is curiously broken up into utterly opposing and contradictory schools. This arises from their failure to agree on a definition of liberty. Anarchism, they all say, is liberty, but what liberty is and how best to secure it are the points on which they divide. The Americans and French say that the liberty of the individual is only logically secured by equal liberty of each to be sovereign only over his own. The Russians say that equal liberty can only be secured by the equal sharing of communism – the individualists retorting that communism swallows up the individual and digests him into the community. Tolstoy says if you adopt altruism as your method and let your brother do what he pleases without resistance, he will let you do what you please and so equal liberty and harmony will come by the law of Christ. Neitzsche says he is Anti-Christ, ridicules and denounces Christianity, altruism, Socialism, equality, communism and social rights, as all equally the inventions of the weak to cheat the strong, declares there is no logical liberty but that of the individual to assert himself thru that struggle for existence and survival of the fittest which is Nature's law, and everything but the law of might will fail.

I, in my writings, did not agree with any of these exactly, but endeavored to effect a reconciliation – a working combination of individualism and communism – the individual to possess and be master of his own personal belongings, but communistic in the larger and social relations.

Again the Anarchists split on the question of property in land. The Individualists held that the only valid title to anything was a labor-title, and as nobody's labor had made the land, therefore it belonged to nobody, but would become the property of whoever occupied and used it just so long as he occupied and used it and no longer. The Communists held that everything belonged to all men equally, the land included. My own proposition was that each man should have a small piece of land, not larger than he could personally occupy and cultivate or use, and a communal right, with all others, in all land not thus individually occupied and used. The Single-Taxers, who, by the way, are largely Anarchistic in theory, agreed with the communists and offered the Single Tax as the best way of equalizing land values and opportunities.

Despite its differences, Anarchism has had a profound and far-reaching influence on human thought. For personal liberty appeals to every brave and original mind. It is to be noted that Anarchists, just as strongly as Marxians, claim to be scientific. Nay, they claim to be more scientific, because they say they would cut away all artificial supports and privileges and leave man absolutely to the natural laws on which alone science bases itself. All governments, they say, are artificial and interfere with Nature. It must be remembered that in their younger days Proudhon and Karl Marx were friends and agreed up to a certain point, where Marx declared the remedy to be to put all social functions under the government, and Proudhon affirmed that government itself, with its privileges and monopolies and invasions of liberty, was the enemy. In those days both called themselves socialists and Marx called himself a Communist, as witness his famous *Manifesto*. Indeed Anarchists still claim to be socialists, a name which the Social-Democrats have no right, they say, to monopolize. All men are socialists, they claim, who are working for the world as it should be, against those who are contented or are contending for the world as it is. They call themselves, sometimes, Free-Socialists, as opposed to what they call State-Socialists – that is, those who would create socialism thru political action.

Now for a little personal history. Our secretary [of a local radical organization], Comrade Zeitelhack will remember that when I offered to join the Westfield Branch, I wrote him I was an Anarchist but as there was no Anarchist Group of Single-Tax party here, and as I believed in radicals working together, I wanted to help the Socialists. He met me on the street and told me he did not think there was much difference in the ultimate aims of Anarchism and Socialism and that he would be glad to have me join, and it was on these terms that I was admitted. I had no thought of becoming a real Socialist, but I studied the thought and the literature and in time came to feel that the Socialists had the best of the argument. Anarchist theories were fine and fascinating, but, as most Anarchists rejected voting, majority rule and even suspicioned organization, they were powerless against the growing evils of capitalism. They refused the ballot because they said the bullet was behind it, but as most of them justified the bullet, at least as a last resort, why not use the ballot? I came to see that government was a tool without which, in some form, cooperative action was impossible. Voting and majority rule were natural necessities of collective functioning, and men could act in no other way if they acted together, and I now saw why, in the twenty years I had been with them, the Anarchists had accomplished nothing except to modify the thought of some of the higher minds. I came to think too that there might be times and places where the rights or necessities of the collectivity might be greater than those of the individual. So I ceased to be an orthodox Anarchist. Nevertheless I have never lost my thirst for personal liberty, only I believe now, that if the Social-Democracy can win, it will give to all men greater practical equal-liberty and security than the vague faiths and method, or no-methods of the Anarchists could achieve.

But I believe that Anarchism and Socialism are both needed in human society – that they represent two strong trends in human psychology – the trend toward liberty and individual variation, and the trend toward cooperation, sympathy and solidarity, and that therefore they should work together. Socialism greatly needs Anarchism as a critic and to keep it from sacrificing the individual and his originality to the domination of the mass. And I have tried, though I confess with no appreciable success, to effect a compromise, which would permit the essential Anarchist principles of Individual Secession and Autonomy of the Group to be guaranteed under Socialism, claiming that if this were done in the Socialistic Constitution and Platforms, the Anarchists would have no logical ground for keeping out of the Party, which would thus gain a multitude of votes – without sacrificing its own principles. Simply an alliance to win, with division of territory and autonomy of method after the conquest of government and the capitalist defeat.

J. Wm. Lloyd

THE DILL PICKLE CLUB

If egoism had a *place*, it was the Dill Pickle Club of Chicago, Illinois. The 1927 edition of *Might is Right* was published by the Dill Pickle Club, as was *The Gospel According to Malfew Seklew*. Jack Jones (d1940) founded the Dill Pickle Club in 1914, his circle of outsiders having outgrown the nearby Radical Book Store.

The Dill Pickle Club was located in Tooker Place, an alleyway that also featured the studio of artist Stanislav Szukalski. An electric green light was placed above the entryway, and the words STEP HIGH STOOP LOW LEAVE YOUR DIGNITY OUTSIDE was painted on the orange-painted door. There were no windows, and the photograph shown here is the only known image of the interior of the Dill Pickle Club. One visitor described it as "a large, comfortable main room with brightly painted chairs and benches, counters along the side where coffee and sandwiches were sold, a small stage—one-act plays were occasionally presented—and a lectern for the night's speaker." (Rideout, *Sherwood Anderson*. University of Wisconsin Press 2005)

In addition to publishing, The Dill Pickle Club hosted amateur plays, costume parties and famously fiery public speaking events. No topic was off limits to praise or criticism, be it homosexuality or religion, communism or anthropology.

In the 1930s Jones refused to pay protection money to the mob / police, and the days of the Dill Pickle Club were soon numbered.

Interior photo of the Dil Pickle Club. Care of The Newberry.

ARTICLES IN THIS SECTION

John Nichols Beffel (1887 — 1973) was a journalist with sympathies toward outsiders and anarchists. Among his many credits are pieces in H. L. Mencken's *American Mercury*, the *Chicago Daily News*, the *Detroit Free Press*, *New Trends*, the *New York World*, and the *New York Herald Tribune*. This sketch of the Dill Pickle Club is from *Cartoons Magazine* Volume 16 Number 6 (December 1911) page 949. *The Gospel According to Malfew Seklew* grants Newton's Law of Gravity third pride of place, following Spencer's Law of the Survival of the Fittest and Darwin's Law of Variation of Species, suggesting it is the Sirfessor himself that Beffel references. Beffel wrote under the names Lancey Fitzgibbons, George Moresby, Mary Starland and Daniel Tower. He emphasis was on anarchist and labor causes such as the Centralia Massacre and the trials of Sacco and Vanzetti. His papers include an unpublished manuscript on anarchist Mikhail Bakunin.

A remarkable excerpt from *Vittles and Vice / An Extraordinary Guide to What's Cooking on Chicago's Near North Side* by Patricia Bronte (Chicago: Henry Regnery Company 1952) with an emphasis on the Dill Pickle Club. The "Stanley Sokolsky" mentioned here is likely the artist Stanislav Szukalski (1893 – 1987).

Up an Alley to a Wild Place
John Nichols Beffel   (1911)

The Dill Pickle Club in Chicago is where visitors from the country and New York are taken to have shivers and shocks. Most of Chicago's best people go there, and all of its worst people.

Lecturers (who once were professors of comparative ethics at the University of Copenhagen or Bayreuth, and are now deans of lunchrooms or prominent night watchmen) deftly set aside the laws of gravitation and attraction, and show where Newton and Galileo were wrong. The drama is dragged upward by the hair of its head, and a successful evening at the club is measured by the number of women who leave before the meeting is half over.

To get to the Dill Pickle, you go through a tight passageway (too narrow for a fat secret service man to get through) into a blind alley, and continue westward till you come to a garbage can. Right alongside this can is the doorway to the club.

One Saturday night a Chicago detective was showing a friend from Kansas City all the tough places in town. Finally, they came in sight of the Dill Pickle Club, where an affinity masquerade was effervescing. The ex-garage in which the club is housed was brilliantly lighted; clouds of cigarette smoke poured from the windows, and the strains of an orchestra almost in tune cleft the night air.

"There's one wild place, Jake," said the detective.

"Tough, eh?" responded the visitor.

"You said it. Every guy that goes into that hall is searched for concealed weapons — and if they find a guy who ain't got any concealed weapons, they give him some."

THE DILL PICKLE CLUB
AND THE SEARCH FOR
"CHICAGO'S GREAT SOUL"
PATRICIA BRONTE   (1952)

When Chicago was the intellectual and literary heart of America —
and incredibly it once was — its nerve center was a rambling old barn
in back of 876 1/2 North Dearborn Parkway, or, more specifically, at
18 Tooker Place. You walked down an alley and found, between two
piles of ash cans, a short narrow door bearing the sign, "Step high,
bend low and leave your dignity behind," and you had arrived at the
Dill Pickle Club.

It lasted from 1917 to 1932, a span of years which marks almost
exactly the rise, decline, and fall of any authentic cultural vigor the
city ever saw, reflecting too the glare of the wild and uproarious
twenties with sound effects by tommy gun.

The Dill Pickle Club started as a high-souled movement of revolution, and the early group included Jack Jones, one of the I.W.W.
founders; poet Carl Sandburg; Jim Larkin and Jack Carney, two Irish
revolutionaries; William Z. Foster and Jack Johnston, two American
Communists; writers Ben Hecht and Alfred Kreymborg; and Stanley
Sokolsky, the sculptor.

Initially, it was the idea of Larkin, a former commander in chief
of the Irish Republican Army and one of the warriors in the Irish
revolution of 1916 headed by Padraic Pearce; he started it in memory
of a Dublin club as a sort of rallying point of young revolutionaries.

But its Moses and leading light from beginning to end was "Dynamiter Jack" Jones, a Canadian-born, sharp-featured, bushy-haired
union organizer, a house painter by trade and creative painter by
hobby. First married to Elizabeth Gurley Flynn, still a well-known
Communist, Jones authored a book called *The Tech-Up*, which became the model plan for the C. I. O. 's industrial unionization. His life
was studded with tragedy; shortly after the advent of the Dill Pickle
Club, Jones married a beautiful young socialite artist. Sailing north
on Lake Michigan for a honeymoon trip, their craft was overturned
in a sudden storm. Jones clung to his bride and the capsized boat for

a herculean eighteen hours, but she was drowned and he near death when aid finally reached them.

The Dill Pickle Club quickly became a hangout for literary and artistic rebels, and the Hobo College crowd moved over from the West Side. It was a hodgepodge, sometimes wild-eyed collection of little theater folk, flappers, society leaders, anarchists, hoboes, and writers, but the most alive and stimulating group ever assembled beneath a Chicago roof. It was, in short, a synthesis, a comradely coming together of the most imaginative and daring souls from every walk of life: the minister met the prostitute, the labor leader knew the editor, the politician met his constituents, the college student found the philosopher, the sociologist studied the criminal, the criminal discovered the beauty of art and perhaps a lawyer, and the writers found treasure beyond belief. The writers included Hecht, shaping his *Thousand and One Afternoons in Chicago*, Sandburg playing his banjo, Charles MacArthur, Manuel Komroff, Theodore Dreiser, Sherwood Anderson, Ring Lardner, Maxwell Bodenheim, Edgar Lee Masters, Vachel Lindsay, Henry Justin Smith, Austin O'Malley, John Drury, and many others; and they were joined by attorney Clarence Darrow, artist Edgar Miller, and actor Richard Bennett, father of Joan and Constance.

The declared intention of the Dill Pickle Club was to "find Chicago's great soul." Another purpose, said Dr. Ben Reitman, long its lecture chairman, was "to elevate the minds of the people to a lower level." He added:

We of the Dill Pickle Club believe in everything. We are radicals, pickpockets, second-story men, and thinkers. Some of us practice free love and free love and some medicine. Many of us have gone through religion and tired of it. Some of us have tired of our wives.

As many as seven hundred people often crowded into the Sunday night lecture meetings, and no topic was barred. Here poets read their own verses; artists talked Dadaism, futuristic abstracts, and Picasso; and experts discussed Vorticism, Freud, psychoanalysis, free love, and companionate marriage. You could get any ideas off your chest, whether you were a paroled convict, a concert musician, an unwed mother, a psychiatrist, a reformed vegetarian, or a three-headed guinea pig. You could advocate murder and arson. In a period when women were revolting against a prudery that was almost obscene in its inversion of truth and lascivious whispering silences, the "inside stuff on sex" was a big draw; the largest crowd that ever attended a lecture came to hear Magnus Hershfield when he discussed sexual abnormalities. It was the heyday of gabby greatness, and a Dill Pickle audience might hear General Coxy (of Coxy's Army), Tom Mooney's brother John, Frederick Cook, the uncrowned discoverer of the North Pole, Chicago Mayor "Big Bill" Thompson, con-man "Yellow Kid" Weil, "Big Bill" Heywood, evangelist Aimee Semple McPherson, Eugene Debs, and Emma Goldman.

The heckling was devastating. If the visitor didn't leave his dignity intact outside, as the motto warned, it was battered beyond recognition inside. The detractors used powerful eloquence, vulgar sarcasm, biting wit, and Marxist logic. Lucy Page Gaston, who came to lecture against cigarettes, said later it was "the most awful adventure of my life." When she was through, Statistical Slim unstuck himself from his chair, opined nastily about reformers in general, then announced: "I never smoked a cigarette in my life. Always been a snuff user. But after hearin' this woman and lookin' into her face, I'm gonna start smokin'. Has anybody got a cigarette?" Then Chairman Reitman ordered two collections taken up, one for the Anti-Cigarette League and the other to buy cigarettes for pacifists then serving jail sentences. Lucy was "infinitely disgusted."

The collections couldn't have amounted to much. The Dill Picklers, gathered about the old pot-bellied stove in their old barn, were a proud proletariat, hugging their poverty. Once, some bandits wandered in and relieved the whole assembly of a total $1.02 except for one embarrassed gentleman who parted with $875.00. The Picklers explained hastily he wasn't a regular.

Lizzie Davis, then queen of the hoboes, once introduced a speaker as "the famous New York gangster who ran Al Capone out of Brooklyn." Even the Dill Picklers were skeptical until they heard later that "Wild Bill" Lovett had been killed in New York. He was wanted for fourteen murders. Lizzie, who wanted to be a writer, knew innumerable gangsters, thieves, prostitutes, con men, and hop-heads. She often sat all night talking with them. Sometimes she didn't talk; she just stayed all night.

In addition to the serious intellectuals, the club attracted a fantastic assortment of guests; it was the rendezvous of high low-brows and low high-brows, long-haired boys and short-haired girls. There was Lena, a little old lady with a poke bonnet and a half-dozen underskirts, widow of the hanged August Spies; Countess Luddie, who wore sandals and bobbed her hair; Van Cina, the Dutch artist vittles and vice and piccolo player; Paddy Caroll from Hell's Half Acre; a Spanish spiritualist who shaved off her hair and dyed her head green; and Reitman, in a frock coat, his red shirt showing beneath a Windsor tie, demanding silence while his wife read her poem, "I Am a Woman, Wee," about standing in the light and looking toward the sun and cosmic love.

Reitman, a physician, an ex-anarchist press agent for Emma Goldman and once a foe of matrimony, also presided over a forum when six young women, "authorities on the subject," discussed the faults and errors of the matrimonially-inclined male.

"Long practice has shown these ladies just where the man falls down when wooing women," explained Reitman.

Once an unmarried pregnant girl was presented for the audience to decide her fate, suicide or abortion, but there are no records of the verdict.

At one time an unnamed patron was going to donate $250,000 for a club building; the first floor was to be used for a forum, a little theater, and a dance hall; the second and third floors would contain rent-free quarters for struggling young artists. The quarter of a million in cash never materialized, but miraculously, the group managed to follow that general plan of action in its ramshackle old carriage house. The Dill Picklers presented plays salvaged from the purgatory shelf which couldn't appear in legitimate theaters: Dreiser's labor drama, The Girl in the Coffin, Pendleton King's Cocaine, Padraic Pearce's The Singer, and a Russian refugee performed Salome and the Dance of the Seven Veils.

Death by violence was no stranger among the Dill Pickle members. In a period of revolt, it occurs among rebels whether there is physical revolution or not. Life and ideas run at a furious pace, and sometimes the pace is too great. One poet got a cop's bullet in the neck while trying to break into a store one night to get paper to write his poems. Another arranged for a drinking wake and then put a bullet in his head. Harry Batter had left an estate of four hundred dollars with instructions to spend fifty dollars to bury him and drink up the balance. It was the most popular wake Chicago ever had.

A minister, Dr. Thornton A. Mills, once pastor of the New England Congregational church at Delaware and Dearborn, in the same block as the Dill Pickle club, constantly defended Jones, and it cost him his parish. To the distaste and alarm of his fashionable flock, he believed that the membership of his wealthy church needed augmenting, and he saw a field of service among the Dill Picklers; he felt they could be brought into his fold and re-educated. His first wife divorced him, and his third suicide try was successful.

Of course the Dill Pickle Club spawned its branch temples. Eddie Clasby opened the Seven Arts Club (among the arts were Vice, Vulgarity, Sacrilege, and Midnight Slumming), Berty Weber's House of Blazes was the most disreputable branch. Big John's Coal Scuttle, Dick Vail's Blue Fish, Berger's House of Correction, and Monty Randall's Montparnasse were all poor imitators. Even today, on North Clark Street, there is a latter-day remnant of the Dill Pickle called the College of Complexes.

The Dill Pickle itself began coming apart at the seams about 1931. The Chicago press had constantly derided them, but conceded at the end that, of the 57 varieties, the Dill Pickle Club was most entertaining. The newspapers accused them of plotting "the over-throw of New York's Greenwich Village and the Latin Quarter in Paris... with pink-shaded lamps, black cats, incense and Turkish cigarettes." Actually, they could afford no fancier trappings than ten-cent egg sandwiches. It was strictly "Art for Art's sake. We're going to make Chicago the center of intellectual expression, the Mecca of the free-minded," they insisted to the last.

The hecklers were supplanted by people who hurled rotten vegetables at the speakers; one night, Dr. Reitman was kidnapped, robbed, and beaten. At the end, members were hounded by cops (Jones had 150 arrest slips the last winter), landlords, gangsters, Prohibition agents, and finally the Internal Revenue department. Through the years, Dill Picklers had constant run-ins with Volstead officials, though there was never any bootlegging; indeed, it was unnecessary, as the visitors brought their own flasks, and Jones sold ginger ale. Then the government revenue men decided, after fifteen years, the club was not "educational" but for profit, though Jack Jones was still yelling his heart out when the final decision came in. But the denouement was a typical Chicago climax: hoodlums tried to horn in and seize control of the club. It started when five gangsters tried to collect a "Capone defense fund"; they wanted to install their mobsters to act as short-change waiters, serve bootleg liquor, and see that the proper crooks got their proper cut. Jones refused to pay vittles and vice off. Suddenly a swarm of city inspectors descended on him and decided he'd been breaking the law for years. Jones finally closed the club himself rather than turn it over to underworld operation.

"Dynamiter Jack" then got a job in a WPA printing project and used to hang around Bughouse Square in the evening, in the shadow of the raucous old glory that was the Dill Pickle Club. He died, broken and unknown, in 1940, followed by Reitman in 1943. The next year there was one last election for the presidency of the non-existent Dill Pickle Club, and one-armed Cholly Wendorf, who is still the Dean of Bughouse Square, won out over Jeff Davis, king of the Hoboes of America, Inc., Jimmy Sheridan of the Sheridan brothers, and Herbert Shaw, the Cosmic Kid.

The moral of this story may be: Chicago has a lot of everything else, but it never had a soul.

THE ANGELS OF THE DILL PICKLE CLUB
TREVOR BLAKE (2017)

Aside from where I stand at any given moment, the *centrum mundi* of egoism in North America is the Dill Pickle Club of Chicago Illinois. Here are excerpts from the *Chicago Tribune* on the rising and falling fortunes of the building where Sirfessor Malfew Seklew and Ragnar Redbeard once held court.

A few words about our cast of characters. Jack Jones was the proprietor of the Dill Pickle Club and the Dill Pickle Press (publisher of the 1927 edition of *Might is Right*). Andrea Hofer Proudfoot (1866 — 1949) founded the League of International Amity in 1913, the Poetry Lovers of America in 1922, and (after World War One) the American Committee for Vienna Relief. She was the author of several books, including *Trolly Lines* (Chicago: R.F. Seymour 1919). Elizabeth Fuller Goodspeed (1893 — 1979) was called "Bobsy" throughout her life. She was the President of the Arts Club of Chicago, a friend of Gertrude Stein and Alice B. Toklas, and was a Chicago socialite. Sidney H. Minchin (1893 — 1951) immigrated to the United States from Germany in 1900. Among other Chicago landmarks, he designed the Storkline Furniture Corporation Factory of Chicago, a building listed in the National Register of Historic Places Program.

Mystery Angel Plots $250,000 Dill Pickle Club
(March 7th, 1920)

A mysterious woman, scion of "one of Chicago's oldest and richest families," is at the bottom of an arch plot to overthrow Greenwich Village and the Latin quarter of Paris as capital of the bohemian world, and make Chicago the ultimate goal of short haired women and men that barbers know not. Within a few years she plans to set up the Dill Pickle Club, that highbrow organization at 18 Tooker place, as the style center of the globe for aesthetic ideas and untrammeled thoughts. There the newer poetry will be born and the higher art will receive its swaddling clothes.

Jack Jones, chief dill among the intellectual pickles, admitted the plot yesterday. He said a woman interested in the club promised to advance $250,000 for the erection of a building containing a "telescopic" theater, a ballroom, and studios where the inspired may be instructed for a nominal sum. The structure will contain four stories and look externally as plain and dilapidated as the most rabid bohemian could desire. The inside, however, is to be a beauty and a joy — all pink shaded lamps and black casts and incense and Turkish cigarettes.

'Angels' of New Dill Pickle Club Abandon Clouds (March 19th, 1920)

The mystery of the feminine "angel" who was to erect a $250,000 building for the dill pickles and give Chicago the world's greatest "Latin quarter" has been solved. [Yesterday] it was discovered there are at least a score of well-to-do folk who will finance the build-structure for the muses to muse in. Among these "angels" are Mrs. Andrea Hofer Proudfoot, author of Trolly Lines and president of the Poetry Lovers of America, Mrs. Elizabeth Fuller, wife of a mine developer in the Porcupine gold fields of Ontario, and Sidney H. Minchin.

The latter has already drawn preliminary sketches of the new building, which he describes as a style suitable for the housing of Dill Pickles. In this structure is to be a ball room, a telescopic theater which will fold up so that even the smallest audience may fill it,

cozy eating places, and a number of studios where instructions will be given to the talented. [...] The success of the building venture will depend, it is claimed, upon a ball to be held tomorrow night at the North Side Turner hall. It is to be an "affinity costume" affair, with the dancers masquerading as milk and cream, squirrel and nut, Antony and Cleopatra, and other great inseparables. There will also be vaudeville and boxing. One thousand dollars must be realized from the ball to obtain an option on the new building site. Then the "angels" will do the rest.

Blaze Damages Printing Plant of Dill Pickles
(October 12th, 1929)

The printing plant of the Dill Pickle club, rendezvous of a so-called Bohemian set at 10 Tooker place, was wrecked yesterday by a fire which for a time threatened to destroy the entire club quarters. Sam Hall, 1216 North Dearborn street, a printer, discovered the blaze and turned in an alarm. Jack Jones, owner of the premises, and manager of the club, estimated the loss at $500.

THE OPTIMIST'S EGO
ANDREA HOFFER PROUDFOOT (1919)

I do not feel me travelling these rails,
Elbowing the herd;
For have I not been chosen to be I?

Some great wise power pruned so well
Through the bloom of teeming life
That I am pleased with this I that I am.
It picked me a keen gray fiery glance
To look out from the lifted mind
It clothed my Self with,
To glimpse all these vistas
That open before me as I ride.

Looking down into the cross-paths
I find the source of this Me that is I
(Which I adore);
I see the vistas of the mother-worlds
Bringing forth I's and I's
To finally fashion just this one
That fits my last and crown so perfectly.

As I press forward into the expanses
Down each passing avenue I look and see
The radiating rows of golden paths
Called for want of better names:
Poetry, Art, Music -
Dawning into the sun-stream
Which happened to be just I;
Dressing the lambent fibers
Which threaded down the pattern into Me.
How perfectly they've come together;
What a choice revelry of dance
They carry on in Me. (Where are we passing?)

So that waking they crowd my longings,
And sleeping they people a world
That I may roam in glory-gleaming ways.
Often I meet John there
And match colors with him,
To prove that the heavenly streets he painted
Were but the poor thoroughfares of his day,
Compared with the endless crosslines
And the intricate composite alleys
That transport us into the glow world
Of the expanded I
Of my day

THE EAGLE AND THE SERPENT.

A Journal of Egoistic Philosophy and Sociology.

"The proudest animal under the sun and the wisest animal under the sun have set out to reconnoitre."—Nietzsche

No. 1.   FEBRUARY 15, 1898.   PRICE THREEPENCE.

THUS SPAKE

NIETZSCHE:
We carry faithfully what we are given, on hard shoulders, over rough mountains! And when perspiring, we are told: "Yea, life is hard to bear!" But man himself only is hard to bear! The reason is that he carrieth too many strange things on his shoulders. Like the camel he kneeleth down and alloweth the heavy load to be put on his back.

EMERSON:
So far as a man thinks, he is free. Nothing is more disgusting than the crowing about liberty by slaves, as most men are, and the flippant mistaking for freedom of some paper preamble like a "Declaration of Independence," or the statute to vote, by those who have never to think or act.

THE EAGLE AND THE SERPENT

The Eagle and the Serpent was a magazine that described itself in several subtitles during its 1898 — 1927 run. These were: "A Journal of Egoistic Philosophy and Sociology," "A Journal of Emersonian Philosophy and Sociology," "A Journal of Wit, Wisdom and Wickedness," "A Journal of Free Spirits and for Spirits struggling to be Free" and "A Quarterly of Egoistic Philosophy and Sociology." Over time it was edited by John Erwin McCall, Malfew Seklew and Richard G. McKnight.

> "A race of altruists is necessarily a race of slaves. A race of freemen is necessarily a race of egoists. Freedom cannot be granted. It must be taken. [...]
>
> Three thousand years of sorrowful experience make the foregoing propositions too evident to us. The object of *The Eagle and the Serpent* is to make them equally evident to all mankind. We stand for the art of life and the life of art–we stand for that freedom which is the life of art and can alone teach us the art of living. When we have converted a body of believers to these views, then our mission will have–begun." —uncredited author, "Our Creed and Aim" from *The Eagle and The Serpent*

The Eagle and The Serpent, No.1, Feb. 1898. Photo of copy owned by S.E. Parker. Care of Sidney E. Parker Archives, sidparker.com.

ARTICLES IN THIS SECTION

A Volcano Has Burst Forth in England

C. L. Swartz (1898)

A "Volcano" has burst forth in England, and the lava that runs down its sides is called *The Eagle and The Serpent*. The responsibility for this rests upon the Eagle Publishing Co., 185 Fleet Street, London, E. C. The price of it (for it is a magazine) is ten cents a copy or sixty cents a year. "Volcano," who guards carefully his identity, had emigrated, it seems, from this country, and he proclaims himself, his bird, and his reptile, followers of Nietzsche and Emerson and various other Egoists. At present the magazine does not present a very harmonious appearance, its heterogeneity resembling somewhat that of our modern day newspapers. Better things may be expected, however, of *The Eagle and The Serpent* after its editor becomes more accustomed to his *ménage*.

A Difference of Words Only
Tak Kak (James L. Walker)　　　　(1888)

To the Editor of *Liberty*:

I think there is no controversy between Mr. J. Wm. Lloyd and myself, though he regards "all acts as Egoistic," while I use the term Egoism, like Stirner, for acts of normal self-possession and self-expression, excluding blind crazes, fanaticism, the influence of fixed ideas, hypnotism dominating the subject and rendering him more of an automaton than of an individual, although he goes through the motions. Rewards and punishments promised and threatened appeal to the Egoism of ignorant believers, but there is also an anti-individualistic craze or fascination in religion, and love, and business, when the idea rides the man. In the last analysis it is a question of sanity or insanity. Egoism is sanity. So we use the term, and as Stirner's book, *Der Einzige und sein Eigenthum*, has long been before the world, his admirers have a good possessory title to this term.

Mr. Lloyd started to sketch the man who "needs to know," but he gives us the portrait of one who has become so far differentiated from the class that now he knows his need, and is actually exercising care in transforming himself, with the — conscious wish and distinct purpose to reach that condition — wherein he will no longer "need to know" at every turn that particular acts are going to be calculably profitable to him. If I admire this man for what he is making of himself, I still imply that I did not admire him for what he was.

A Dream of Beyond—All-Too-Beyond, Woman
Volcano (John Basil Barnhill)   *(1897)*

"I slept and dreamed that life was beauty, I woke and found that life was duty."

No, not duty but — tragedy. I dreamed that social reformers no longer found the words of Coleridge a true description of their success with women:

"It seems a story from the world of spirits,

If any one obtains that which he merits

Or any merits that which he obtains."

I dreamed that the handsomest, loveliest, women lavished all their charms and favors upon plumb-liners, ruthlessly boycotting all reactionaries and conservatives. Alas, it was a dream.

Again I slept and dreamed that men and women were at last appreciated at their true worth and value, that is according to their ability to make the opposite sex happy.

The saint and hero was that one who could make twenty of the opposite sex happy. Such dreams are strands in the rope which connects us with beyond-man. — Arrows of longing for beyond-woman. Man yet will say :

I slept and dreamed that life was duty,

I woke and found that life was beauty.

A Unanimous Conviction
VOLCANO (JOHN BASIL BARNHILL)   (1897)

The other day I passed by a large and apparently flourishing rock pile whereon many of my brothers were working with shameless lack of enthusiasm. One of these I recognized as belonging to a highly respectable family. To him I said, "does not your uncle have a most successful establishment at the sign of the three golden balls — surely he would give you a lift?" He turned on me a gaze of inexpressible anguish and replied: "He is my brother, but he will not help me. He said to me that my life was a damned failure, and that I was only fit for the rock pile."

"Then the banker millionaire around the corner, he also is your brother; surely he will help you." "No" he replied, "he calls me a — damned failure." "But your brother in Italy who has grown fabulously rich in selling pieces of the true cross, he will help you."

"No, he too calls me a damned failure. Perhaps you do not know that Solomon is only an assumed name."

"Pray who are you then?"

"I am Jesus of Nazareth."

"Then I am compelled to say that your life has been a damned failure."

"Thou almost persuadest me to cease being a Christian" he said.

"Go," were his last words to me, "go into all the world and preach the salvation of Egoism to the children of men. Say to them that you saw Jesus of Nazareth on the rock (pile) of Mount Calvary and that by the unanimous opinion of all Altruists and Egoists he was adjudged a damned failure; that he does not wish to deceive the children of men any longer, but admits in the face of all the world that the greatest blunder and crime hitherto committed on earth has been my teaching, live for others. Tell them that on the rock pile, of my martyrdom I now meditate with tears of joy on Zarathustra's new teaching which saith: Your love for your neighbor is your bad love for yourselves... Ye flee from yourselves unto your neighbor and would fain make a virtue thereof; but I see through your 'unselfishness.' The thou is older than the I; the thou hath been proclaimed holy but the I not yet. I counsel you not to love your neighbor but to love those who are the most remote... One must learn how to love one's self with a whole and healthy love, that one may find life with one's self endurable and not go gadding about... Such a gadding about baptizeth itself 'love unto one's neighbor...' Verily it is no commandment for today and tomorrow to learn how to love one's self. It is rather the finest, cunningest, last and most patient of arts... The man of perception must not only be able to love his enemies but also to hate his friends... Be sure to love your neighbor as yourselves — but first of all be such as love themselves — as love themselves with great love, with great contempt... My great love unto the most remote commandeth: 'Spare not your neighbor.' Man is a something that must be surpassed... Your work is your neighbor. 'This — is my way — where is yours?'... In the end one experienceth nothing but one's self... I ask you to lose me and find yourselves... Nobody telleth me new things so that I telleth mine own self unto myself... He loveth his enemies but he taketh revenge for that on his friends."

MARGINALIA
THE NEW AGE   (1907)

Now that Nietzsche has entered the sphere of general discussion it is natural that publishers should find a growing demand for works dealing with the philosophy of Egoism, and Mr. Fifield is doing a service by issuing a translation of Max Stirner's *The Ego and His Own*. This is the first translation of Stirner to be published in England. Will the next move on these lines be the issue of some of the works of Ragnar Redbeard?

∉

Max Stirner is of course pre-Nietzschean, the above-mentioned work having first appeared in his native country, Germany, about sixty years ago. English readers, however, have had an opportunity in recent years of making acquaintance with his views by means of translations issued in America, where there always seems to be a public for ideas which are just off the beaten track.

∉

It is not generally known that there is quite a literature Egoism in the States. True, it is not always of the best order, but it is quite good at its best and genuinely amusing at its worst. Some of the periodicals devoted to its study are fearfully and wonderfully made; one of these was called *I*, but whether it still asserts itself, or whether it has gone the way of many inferior sheets I do not know.

∉

England has had but one consciously and deliberately egoistic journal. *The Eagle and the Serpent* and it led a chequered and fitful career in the later eighteen-nineties and the early nineteen-hundreds. Its sixteen octavo pages sometimes appeared in the conventional typographical form, " justified" at each side, at others the right-hand side of the page tailed off like type-writing, giving the print the appearance of blank verse. It was in these pages, however, that many English people first learned of Nietzsche, for, besides freely quoting and discussing this philosopher, one number contained Thomas Common's translation of the "Prefatory Discourse" of *Zarathustra*.

∉

The Eagle and the Serpent was always fortunate in its correspondence. It had eminent readers and a valuable trick of beguiling them into its controversies. In this way, it managed to print letters from many of the leading modern thinkers, among whom may be mentioned Alfred Russel Wallace, Bernard Shaw, W. H. Mallock, Ernest Newman, E. H. Crosby, Benjamin Kidd, and Morrison Davidson. These letters were dealt with under the heading "Benedictions and Maledictions," and with the numerous and excellent quotations from Nietzsche, Stirner, Rochefoucauld, Montaigne, Thoreau, and others, which formed a liberal part of the paper, *The Eagle and the Serpent* was well worth the threepence asked for it.

FRIEDRICH NIETZSCHE

Friedrich Nietzsche (1844 – 1900) is exceptionally well documented elsewhere, and *Der Geist* has very little to add. For the few who some-how see his name here first, here is that very little. Nietzsche was a philosopher and an author born in Prussia. In *Thus Spoke Zarathus-tra* (1883), Nietzsche wrote of the overman, one whose right comes from his might. In *Beyond Good and Evil* (1886), he wrote of the indi-vidual and not external moralities as the basis for ethics. In *The Anti-christ* (1888), he wrote of the destruction of religion by men willing to say God is dead.

Nietzsche was never asked if he had read Stirner, and he nev-er wrote that he had read Stirner. It seems possible Nietzsche read Stirner. After more than a century of debate on the possibility that Nietzsche read Stirner, *Der Geist* offers the final judgement: *it doesn't matter*. Let us read and consider both in their similarities and their differences. Egoists and Overmen who ignore their ego and their will in favor of a mere pedigree are confused from the start. Most of our "Union of Egoists" (Seklew, Redbeard, Tucker, *et. al.*) freely sang of either or both according to their own purposes.

ARTICLES IN THIS SECTION

"Nietzsche" has not been reprinted since its first appearance in Clarence Lee Swartz's journal *I*
Number 5 (January 1898). Gordak appeared in three issues of *The Eagle and The Serpent*.

An exchange first published in the magazine *T. P.'s Weekly*. "T. P." was Thomas Power O'Connor
(1848 — 1929), journalist and MP in the House of Commons. T. P.'s Weekly was published from
1902 to 1924. The subject of the exchange is proper credit for the earliest printed English-language translations of Friedrich Nietzsche. Thomas Common, John Barnhill, A. G. Field and the
egoist magazine they appeared in — *The Eagle and The Serpent* — are all given their due.

NIETZSCHE

WILLIAM WALSTEIN GORDAK   _(1898)_

I sneezed, —it was his name;
  He is a great philosopher,
But then, —I am the same,
  And deal much less in metaphor.

I am not overmuch
  In love with overmen;
Who hanker after such
  Are simple folk, but then—

If think they that he meant
  Themselves the overclod,
That is quite different,
  Much different, God Lord!

NIETZSCHE IN *T. P.'S WEEKLY*

Bernard Lintot (May 2nd 1913):

In the preface to the final volume of the edition, Dr. Oscar Levy pays a fine tribute to those who have worked with him on the production of the eighteen volumes. And he gives in the following passage a brief history of the efforts to introduce Nietzsche into England:

> It was in the year 1893 that Nietzsche's name is first mentioned in one of the books of the unfortunate English poet John Davidson. In the following year a group of German, English, and Scottish admirers of Nietzsche arranged to bring out an authorised version of the German thinker's works, three volumes of which were actually published in 1896 and 1897. The reception of these books was so discouraging that no further arrangements could be made by the publishing firm, which shortly afterwards, owing chiefly to the extensive liabilities incurred by the Nietzsche edition, had to give up business. In the next six years — from 1897 to 1903 — in spite of various endeavours by some indefatigable defenders of the faith, it was found absolutely impossible to get a hearing for Nietzsche either with the public, the Press, or the publishers. Their hopes went down to freezing-point when, in 1903, *The Dawn of Day* was given to the public, only to meet again with a cold reception. But in 1907 the party had somewhat recovered its spirit, and as a last experiment brought out a translation of *Beyond Good and Evil* — this time at private risk, for no publisher could be induced to take up an author twice repudiated. This translation was one which had been made nearly ten years ago, but until then had never seen, and was never expected to see, the light of publicity. It turned out to be a success — a half-hearted success perhaps, but one that at last told the few inmates of the Nietzschean ark that the waters of democracy had diminished, and that at least some higher peaks of humanity were free from the appalling deluge. The success encouraged them once more to take up their old project of the publication of the same first four volumes of this, the present translation, left the press and were favourably received, though yet by a small

and none too enthusiastic public. Towards the end of the same year three more volumes were published. In 1910 and 1911 the remaining ten volumes of the translation appeared, while most of the previously published volumes went into a second and even a third edition. No volume was published in 191 2, but with the index the last and, as is to be hoped, a very useful volume is added to this, the most complete and voluminous translation of any foreign philosopher into the English language.

In the above passage Dr. Oscar Levy does not, of course, set out to write a complete history of the development of interest in Nietzsche in this country. But I think he might have mentioned the pioneer work done by the first and only journal devoted to the Nietzschean philosophy ever published in this country, *The Eagle and The Serpent*. And I think he is wrong also in imagining John Davidson to be the first English writer to mention Nietzsche. I do not know to whom the honour will be finally due, but I do know that "George Egerton" (Mrs. Golding Bright) mentions the philosopher in *Keynotes*, which was first published in the year 1892.

A. G. Field (May 23rd, 1913):

Friedrich Nietzsche in England
To the Editor of *T. P.'s Weekly*
Sir, – The generous reference by Bernard Lintot, in *T. P.'s Weekly* of May 2nd, to the early promulgation of Nietzschean principles by the magazine *The Eagle and the Serpent*, will bring happiness to at least one heart. Stretched on his sick-bed in a Washington hospital, threatened with desquamative nephritis, lies at this moment John Basil Barnhill, one of literature's pioneers; one of those who penetrate axe in hand into the thickets of popular ignorance. Such men gain nothing for themselves, except the jungle fevers and the warrior's wounds and hunger. Among a crowd of original and valuable ideas moving him to a perpetual action, two were most persistent — a desire to place Bizet on his proper plane among thinkers as well as among musicians, and an unconquerable resolution to bring Nietzsche into the ken of the English-speaking peoples.

Well do I remember his translations of and writings on Nietzsche, for I myself made some of the former and circulated many of the latter. Bernard Lintot gives due and adequate praise to the monumental work of Dr. Levy, but he rightly adds some corrections to Dr. Levy's curious notes on the early work in connection with Nietzsche. Why is Thomas Common so absolutely ignored? But there were prophets even before Common. Among the hardy few none more full of the radiancy of hope and courage than John Basil Barnhill, who finally, in the pages of *The Eagle and the Serpent*, attempted to popularise the Neitzschean philosophy. When he saw that the pioneer work was over, and that the "morning red" had indeed dawned over England, he stopped his journal and commenced his pioneer work on Vauvenargues, Rivarol, and Chamfort. The first English translation of any quantity of Chamfort's caustic epigrams was made by me and issued by Barnhill in the pages of one of his ephemeral magazines. This quixotic spirit was all the while on Bizet, reading the deepest philosophical meaning into the junction of his striking musical ideas with a plot taken from Merimée's novel. Readers of *T. P.'s* already know that when Nietzsche broke with Wagner on the ground of that composer's apostasy from a pagan dramatic movement to a Christian, or "slave," principle, he attempted to aggrandise Bizet and particularly Bizet's great work, *Carmen*, at the expense of Wagner. Those wrangles seem singularly old and dead to us to-day; yet the conviction that something unappreciated in Bizet rests yet to be brought home to the people inspires Barnhill on his sick-bed. He writes me from the hospital:—

> If this ward were provided with an orchestra playing *Carmen*, or even a gramophone reading Maupassant's *On Merimée's* inimitable stories to me, I could tolerate it and get well. As it is I am still thinking out — not working at it very much, that is at present impossible — my great work on Bizet, I have now reached the section *Carmen Nights* — a series of tragic tales told me by the world's wastrels whom I have taken on various occasions to hear the opera. A veritable *Magnificat* of Bizet. No really sympathetic life of him exists in English. Of course, he got a stupendous puff from Nietzsche, and others from Runciman: 'The second act is so brilliant that it positively sheds light." Can you help me to assemble the critiques of the French and Germans who have appreciated Bizet's greatness? Perhaps this is a lifelong task I am suggesting?

And so the untiring brain works on, on — always engaged in some unbusinesslike and non-paying proposition; always offering its

Friedrich Nietzsche

service to humanity and sacrificing to the manes of the neglected and unappreciated.

Barnhill is assailed by a fear that his present illness may develop into something fatal, but he faces it as boldly as he has faced other contingencies almost as terrible. Finding his principles, Nietzschean and other, discordant with a professional position from which he was drawing a comfortable salary, he abandoned not his principles but his salary. To-day he writes:—

> Doctors say this is probably Bright's disease. I have accepted the challenge of Mr. Bright and I intend to fight him to a finish. Personally, I think I may come out victor, if not, well—as Brutus says:
> Therefore, our everlasting farewell take—
> For ever, and for ever, farewell, Cassius!
> If we do meet again, why, we shall smile;
> If not, why then, this parting was well made.

It is not remarkable that Barnhill's pioneer work for Nietzsche, which I, a Socialist and anti-Nietzschean, declare to have been of the first importance to the thinking world, should have been neglected. He belongs to the class who are always, partly through their own defects of advertising ability, neglected and ignored. His father fought and died in the American Civil War, and yet he draws no pension, in a land where the distinction consists in not having a pension. He has lectured and fought for the Democratic party for twenty years, and now the party is in power it does not even offer him a vice-consulship, say, at Leeds, Cardiff, or Bristol, where his old friends and fellow pioneers could see him and hear the old accents.

A few of those who have read this man's writings, or even who now hear of his work for the first time, might like to send him a line of affection and encouragement. In that case I would be glad to forward it, or give any necessary information.

A. G. FIELD 28, Ilminster Gardens, S.W.

Oscar Levy (May 30th, 1913):

Dr. Oscar Levy and Nietzsche Pioneers
Sir, — I am very much obliged to Mr. A. G. Field for drawing, my attention to Mr. John Basil Barnhill, the former editor of *The Eagle and*

the Serpent, the earliest Nietzschean periodical in England. I knew of this periodical, but not of its editor.

At the same time — as Mr. Bernard Lintot in his generous appreciation of my Nietzsche translation already suggested — I was only giving a. short retrospective sketch of "The Nietzschean Movement in England" in my introductory essay to the index volume of the Nietzsche translation. I did not intend to write a historical survey of the whole movement, for the simple reason that I could not have done it, even if I had tried. I have no knowledge f. i. [for instance] of Mr. J. B. Barnhill and his work. The only competent person to do justice to this task would be my friend Mr. Thomas Common, of Edinburgh, who from the beginning has taken an active and leading part in the movement, which I myself only joined at a much later state.

It would, therefore, have been more than ungrateful on my part if, as Mr. A. G. Field suggests, I had tried to ignore in my preface Mr. Thomas Common, of whom I knew. If I may be allowed to refer Mr. A. G. Field to page 21 of this preface, he will see that I paid my tribute not only to Mr. Thomas Common, but likewise to Mr. William Haussmann for their steadfast and courageous work in our cause. Both Mr. Common and Mr. Haussmann (who is a German-American living in Philadelphia) stood sponsor for the first edition of Nietzsche, with which I myself had nothing to do. This edition, published by Henry and Co. and later on by Fisher Unwin, had unfortunately to be discontinued. But both Mr. Common and Mr. Haussmann have likewise given active and generous help to my edition, and to omit their names would have been on my part decidely unjust, or what is called in English "unsportsmenlike."

OSCAR LEVY

Thomas Common (June 6th 1913):

To the Editor of *T. P.'s Weekly*
Sir, — One is obliged to Mr. Field for giving us news — alas! it is sadness! — about Mr. Barnhill (Erwin McCall), who issued *The Eagle and Serpent* in the early Nietzschean days. Mr. Field, though he has evidently been a coadjutor of Mr. Barnhill, seems to have been too modest in those days, for I do not think his name appeared in *The Eagle and Serpent*. All honour however to Mr. Field and Mr. Barnhill for spreading a knowledge of N.'s philosophy and ideas in those early days. Our best

wishes also for Mr. Barnhill's speedy restoration to health.

When one examines closely the introductory essay in Vol. XVIII of N.'s works, one must admit that the criticisms of Messrs. Lintot and Field are justified to a considerable extent. In spite of some ambiguity, one naturally infers that it is meant that Mr. John Davidson was the first person to make reference to N. in the English language — even as late as 1893.

Vixere fortes ante Agamemnona multi.

So far as I know, the first reference (quite favourable) to N. in English is as far back as 1877, in an article on "Philosophy in Germany" in *Mind* 11 p. 493. The first person, so far as I know, to translate anything of N.'s writings into English was Helen Watterson whose version of twelve of N.'s aphorisms was published in the *Century Magazine* (New York) in May, 1859. The *Review of Reviews* soon began to mention N. in its notices of the foreign periodicals — e.g., in April 1891, when it called attention to an important article on N. in *Nord und Sud*. So far as I know, the first independent article on N. in an English periodical appeared in the *Speaker* for November 28th, 1891. A virulent attack on N. appeared in the *International Journal of Ethics* for July 1892. When, however, the very able article on N., by G. Valbert, appeared in the *Revue des Deux-Mondes* for October 1st, 1892, and was noticed with some fairness by the *Review of Reviews* for November, there was no longer any excuse for cultured Englishmen remaining ignorant of N.'s principles. Numerous references to N. then began to appear.

One cannot however to justice to all the Nietzschean pioneers; we should not however neglect Mr. Schumm, whose translations of many of N.'s aphorisms appeared at an early period in B. Tucker's *Liberty*. Mr. John Badcock should also be remembered. He added long quotations from N. to his *Slaves to Duty*.

It would require another long letter to explain how the English translation of N. has been delayed for about a dozen years or more. It was certainly not the indifference of the public, the press, and the publishers which was the main cause of the long delay.

Yours faithfully, THOMAS COMMON.

Whitehouse Terrace, Corstorphine, N. B.

Bernard Lintot (June 6th 1913):

On another page of this issue a letter apepars from Mr. Thomas Common in further contribution to the discussion on the early pioneers of Nietzsche in Great Britain raised three weeks ago on this page. All who are acquainted with the progress of the Nietzsche philosophy in this country realise how much we owe to Mr. Thomas Common. It was largely due to his interest in the subject that Nietzsche was introduced to the British public in the middle of the eighteen-nineties; and above all he is the author of the best English translation of *Thus Spoke Zarathustra*, Nietzsche's greatest work, and in the opinion of the *Encyclopaedia Britannica* "the most original philosophic and poetic masterpiece of modern German literature." "The Prefatory Discourse" of this work, translated by Mr. Common, originally appeared in *The Eagle and The Serpent*, and afterwards Mr. William Reeves issued in 1902 a volume containing his translation of Part I of the book. The complete translation by Thomas Common appears in Dr. Oscar Levy's edition of Nietzsche's works. In 1903 Mr. Common began to issue a little Nietzchean quarterly entitled *Notes for Good Europeans*, but before that he had issued a volume entitled *Nietzsche as Critic, Philosopher, Poet, and Prophet / Choice Selections from His Works*, with a portrait of Nietzsche and introduction, through Mr. Grant Richards, besides other translations.

FREE SPIRITS

11

The Eagle and The Serpent (1898 — 1927) was for a time published with the subtitle "A Journal of Free Spirits and for Spirits struggling to be Free." *The Eagle and The Serpent* quotes Joseph A. Labadie in issue 18 (circa 1902), and his son Laurance Labadie used "A Journal for Free Spirits" as the subtitle for his own *Discussion* journal in 1936. Laurance in turn was an influence on Mark A. Sullivan, who chose the same subtitle for his own gay individualist anarchist publication *The Storm* in 1976. In this same spirit, *Der Geist* collects "free spirits" too individualistic for other sections of our journal.

Sidney E. Parker sitting on a patio overlooking a garden, reading the paper.
Date & location unknown. Care of Sidney E. Parker Archives, sidparker.com.

ARTICLES IN THIS SECTION

My Journey to the Sidney E. Parker Archives
Kevin I. Slaughter   (2018)

It seems appropriate for me to begin by telling you about myself, because it will shed light on the why part of this story. Then I can deal
with the who, what, where and when that these tales are supposed
to include. It will all necessarily be fragments, what I can remember,
what I was able to find documentation of.

∉

As I write this, I am in my early-40s. I have always been predisposed
to egoism,[1] though I didn't always have the same language or con-
ceptual framing of it that I do now. I explicitly considered myself an
atheist and individualist in the mid-1990s, being drawn to the he-
retical, skeptical, anti-egalitarian, and entertaining writings of An-
ton Szandor LaVey and H.L. Mencken.[2] Both of these men served as
a gateway to *most* of the interests I have today. Egoism as a world-
view on its own has been largely neglected by scholars, with only a
handful of writers who have dealt with it in anything more than a
cursory fashion. Because John Henry Mackay, the first archivist and
historian of egoism was an anarchist, Max Stirner has inextricably
been linked with anarchism. I was never much interested in anarchism, because I was never exposed to any of the potentially interesting writers, mostly just angry confused kids and corporate co-option.

∉

In mid-2009 I made a note for myself: "need to read Max Stirner
more frequently." For the life of me, I cannot remember in what context that was said. I *do* know that I did not follow those instructions
to myself for many years, but when I did...

∉

Some time in mid-2010 I began promoting the writing of Benjamin
DeCasseres, an egoist poet and journalist with a flair for the Satanic.
I found DeCasseres by way of H. L. Mencken, picking up a copy of
DeCasseres' book *Mencken and Saw: The Anatomy of America's Voltaire*

---

1   My egoism may not be your egoism, but it is mine, and it's the only true
egoism because it is mine.
2   Both of them, of course, influenced by Friedrich Nietzsche, whose writings
I read as well, but which were not as approachable to me as the two American writers.

and England's Other John Bull[3] along with some more Mencken and a Ben Hecht at a local library sale in December, 2009. Mencken first championed DeCasseres in the pages of *The Smart Set*, the journal Mencken and George Jean Nathan edited before they started *The American Mercury* in 1924. It was in the pages of the latter that I discovered a passion for the writings of both DeCasseres and the Irish hobo author Jim Tully.[4] Later that year I discovered and devoured Mencken's *Men versus The Man*, a strident defense of individualism against collectivism. It was clear, though, why this brilliant, biting and often hilarious work by Mencken was no longer in print, and therefore eluded me for so long. I published a new edition of *Men versus The Man* in November of 2011.[5]

2012

By April 2012 I had discovered the journal *The Eagle and The Serpent*. It was astounding, life altering, in a real sense. I never imagined there could be a *group* of Nietzschean-inspired writers who saw the world in a way I did, over 120 years ago. The journal explicitly championed Nietzsche, Emerson, Thoreau, Stirner. I still had little substantive knowledge of Max Stirner, though Benjamin DeCasseres mentioned him often, so I was *aware* of him. In December 2012 I published *A Bible Not Borrowed from the Neighbors: Essays and Aphorisms on Egoism,* a book largely culled from the *The Eagle and The Serpent*.[6] It was the first time I had associated my name in print with the word "Egoism" and the beginning of my study of the work of Max Stirner himself, *A Bible Not Borrowed...* was released within two days of Sidney E. Parker's death, though I wouldn't know that for a few more years.

I was vaguely familiar with Sidney Edward Parker. He'd written

---

3   It is on the very first page of that book we see the geist of Stirner: "...an Individualist says, 'My Ego against the world!'" (New York: Silas Newton 1930)

4   I was flabbergasted to discover in 2017 that Jim Tully was featured in a relaunched 1927 American edition of *The Eagle and Serpent* (the title slightly different), edited by Richard G. McKnight with the assistance of Malfew Seklew.

5   I had published an edition of Mencken's translation of Nietzsche's *The Anti-Christ* in 2008.

6   It was just shortly before publishing A Bible Not Borrowed... that I discovered the just-released Ardent Press book *Enemies of Society: An Anthology of Individualist & Egoist Thought*. It was significantly culled from the journals of Sidney E. Parker, though there is a great deal of material from other sources as well, including new writing. It contained two works that I'd already chosen to include in my book. I noted that, and made a hearty recommendation of Enemies of Society.

an introduction to one of my favorite books, *Might is Right*. I'd read that introduction probably once, in the early 1990s. It was Redbeard that I was really interested in. Of course, on reflection I wish I'd paid more attention to Sid, but I didn't.

2016

When Trevor Blake and I started the Union of Egoists project in February of 2016,[7] Parker's name came up again. And again. *And again.* It quickly became apparent that S. E. Parker was *very* important to what Trevor and I were doing. We set up UnionOfEgoists.com to focus on a core of 6 figures: Trevor Blake, Benjamin DeCasseres, Dora Marsden, Ragnar Redbeard, Malfew Seklew and Max Stirner. They basically represented what we thought were the most interesting egoists, to us. I was particularly interested in DeCasseres[8] and Redbeard, Trevor in Marsden and Seklew, and both of us in Stirner, naturally. But then we couldn't just ignore all of the other fascinating people influenced by and promoting an egoism inspired by Stirner. And Sid *kept coming up*. February 5th of 2016 I shot Trevor Blake a message via a messenger app:

02-05 KEVIN SLAUGHTER: Sidney Parker alive?

02-05 TREVOR BLAKE: I have tried to find that out myself, and I don't know.

Trevor Blake and I use the messenger app heavily. Every day, through the day, messages about the project flow. Since we've used it from the start of the project it has become an indispensable resource for documenting our work. The next day I got a bit of useful information and shot it over to Trevor:

02-06 KS: S. E. Parker died in 2012 [...]

02-07 KS: Is there no single S. E. Parker resource online? Sheesh. Dead only 4 years!

02-08 TB: I found little and what I found was small and scattered.

---

7   The Union of Egoists project was formally announced on April 1st, 2016.
8   I'd been running BenjaminDeCasseres.com since 2012 and have been reprinting DeCasseres' work since then as well.

Two comrades in London were also on the case. Pól O'Sullivan is the egoist historian who wrote an introduction to the lost interview between Parker and Tony Gibson from 1993. I regularly consult with Pól and he's been integral to the Sidney E. Parker Archives and Union of Egoists. Pól and another comrade, Jeff, were meeting as the London Union of Egoists. Without the two of them, and without a trace of hyperbole or exaggeration, all of Sid's belongings would be in the garbage right now.

> 02-08 KS: (quoting Pól) "I think he was still married and living in Notting Hill at the time of his death. What I didn't know is that he had a son who had been brought up in a care home... He must have had correspondence going back to the 1950s with various luminaries of anarchist individualism. What has become of this collection is anybody's guess." [...]

> 03-28 KS: Jesus... Parker published DeCasseres in 1965...[9] [...]

> 03-29 KS: So, I think two names are missing from UoE: Parker and Novatore. [...]

> 03-30 KS: There is a Sidney Parker page on Facebook that 4 people "like"[10] that was created by my man in London. He just made me an admin, so if we do any S. E. Parker stuff we can post from there as well.

Svein Olav Nyberg published an egoist journal first titled *non-serviam* and later titled *i-studies*. Issues 13 and 14 of *non serviam*, released to celebrate the 150th anniversary of the publication of *Der Einzige und sein Eigentum,* are the last issue of Sid's journal *EGO.*[11] Sid passed the metaphorical torch to Svein and Svein has passed it along to the Union of Egoists & *Der Geist*.

---

9   Later I would find that he quotes DeCasseres earlier on the cover of his non-political journal *Twice* published in 1963.

10   It's almost at 80 as of this writing. Seems Sid is still an obscure figure.

11   It also announced the completion of the first ebook edition of *The Ego and His Own*, compiled and edited by Nyberg *et. al.*

04-04 KS: ...I hit (Nyberg) up with an inquiry about the Parker estate:
I'm in touch with a few fellows in London, who have met up twice now as a Union of Egoists. One was in touch with Sidney Parker before he died and obviously you had some communication with him. ...I've been terribly concerned with the status of the Parker estate and one of my London contacts has been considering swinging by the last known address.
For such a prominent egoist who was alive so recently, I'm bothered by how difficult it is to get his work.

$\notin$

I first contacted Bernd A. Laska on April 4th. Bernd runs the LSR website where he publishes material dedicated to three writers. "LSR" is Julien Offray de La Mettrie, Max Stirner, and Wilhelm Reich. I was trying to find out if Bernd had control over the domain nonserviam. com. He didn't. I also mentioned Sid. Bernd ended his email: "Do you know when Sid Parker died? Died he at all? Obituaries?"

04-04 KS: oooft... he doesn't control the domain... so basically it's up in the air.
also, incredibly sad that nobody actually seems to know when Parker died. [...]

04-06 KS: From Nyberg: "Ken MacLeod (who lives in Edinburgh) also tried to contact his estate, but to no avail. Your best bet is his son Leon Parker."
Note, though, that Leon was not on speaking terms with his parents after adulthood. Sid was, from what is said, «worse than a poor father».
None the less, I would hope his musings were rescued for posterity."

On April 7th I found Leon online. I was writing to Chip Smith of Nine-Banded Books[12] about it all. Chip asked if I had a copy of the Jean Pierre Schweitzer booklet *O Idios: Three Essays on Individualist Anarchism* which Sid spoke of in the 1993 interview. "I don't have

---

12   www.ninebandedbooks.com

ANY S. E. Parker published material, just his stuff in other journals / books" I responded. I barely knew Sid's work at the time, to be honest, I only knew *I had to know more*, and that Sid had already done, for decades, what I was doing now. I only knew that, like me, he was a fan of Ragnar Redbeard and Benjamin DeCasseres and Max Stirner.

I composed my first letter to Leon, introducing myself and name-dropping Nyberg, and letting him know I was doing some research on his father. I wasn't ready for the response.

"My Mother is still alive I only met again after 38 years when my father died" he said in a message, "she is back to not communicating with me." He was very forthcoming about everything. "As for my father he was cremated without permission by Westminster council and his ashes are sitting on a shelf in a crematorium.[13] Perhaps my Mother still feels the times he beat her and broke her ribs has done nothing with his remains?"

I didn't want to deal with the human stuff. I rolled my eyes, and it put a damper on following up. I try to avoid being involved in stranger's lives as much as possible but some amount is unavoidable. I did not idolize Sid, nor would I. I am not a religious devotee but one who tries to understand there is no perfection in this world, and there is no next world for it to be in.

"I am interested in also looking the issues of libertarians like my parents being crap parents," Leon said. I get it, and maybe there is something there. I hadn't done any thinking on the subject but there is precedent for ideologically driven people to be shitty with family stuff. An analogy I've used before is how so many eugenicists ended up having no children of their own.

I tried focusing on just discussing "getting Sid's stuff," but still lending a sympathetic ear as much as seemed *needed*. At that point Leon's mother Pat still lived in the flat. Leon told me that he'd been estranged from his parents for many years, but then his mother reached out to him when Sid died and they reunited. He would come around and do tasks for her, like go to the grocery store. I believe that lasted only a few months before she cut him off again. I also began talking to Leon's daughter as well, who seemed a little more stable. Her biological mother is long out of the picture, and Leon's last wife

---

13   The ashes were later retrieved and scattered in a memorial garden north west of London.

Sid's former flat in September 2016, where his wife Pat
had lived alone for 4 years after his death.

also has moved back overseas, where she's from.

Leon would sell records at what we would call "flea market"... he had a stall somewhere. I think he had a job at a record store as well, or at one time... It's unclear and I tried not to ask too many personal questions. I imagine that he probably relied heavily on the state, as he lived in a "council house" and was basically a ward of the state his whole life.

> 04-17 KS: Our man in London: "Looks like me and Jeff will probably meet up with Leon in the next 7-10 days. Not sure what will transpire, but it's a start."

⊄

Near the end of April I made contact with the Labadie Collection at the University of Michican to obtain scans of Sid's last journal *En Marge*. Only two issues were ever released in 1995 and '96.

I never attended a University and had not engaged in the type of research that involved University libraries. In the few short years since this contact I've engaged dozens of libraries around the world.

The Labadie Collection sent the scans and I released a facsimile edition of *En Marge* No. 1 as the first in a new publishing series Trevor and I named *Stand Alone*. 99 copies were made on three different papers, and given away for free. 33 from a distro in the UK, 33 from Little Black Cart, and 33 from my own distro Underworld Amusements.

Just last month (Sepember 2018) the Union of Egoists released the 24th installement in that series: *The New En Marge*. It contained a facsimile of issue number 2 of Sid's last journal.

⊄

I first spoke with Leon by Skype while visiting Trevor in Portland for a May 1st book release reading[14] at Mother Foucault's bookstore.[15] I was putting off the call because Leon kept mentioning being abandoned, and his rough childhood in his emails and, well... dang, I just didn't want to have to have that conversation... but learning that Sid's stuff may indeed still be there, and that it may contain decades of correspondences with egoists and other fascinating individuals, and copies of his hard-to-find journal, and maybe manuscripts of

---

14   *Outbursts of Everett True* by A.D. Condo and J. W. Raper, and *Max Stirner Bibliography* by Trevor Blake.

15   MotherFoucaultsBookshop.com

things never published, well... I had to see it through. I'd discovered in my research that one of the items, for example, was an item Mark A. Sullivan[16] announced in *The Storm:* the forthcoming publication of an English translation of the *Protagoras, Nietzsche, Stirner* by Benedict Lachmann, originally published in Germany in 1914. It was going to be paired with another original translation on Stirner. It was to be released in the mid-80's but never was. As far as I could tell, it

---

16   Sullivan published the egoist journal *The Storm* that published the essay by Sidney E. Parker that would later become the introduction to *Might is Right*.

I   Protagoras

There are few philosophical problems as important for the general public as the problem of ethics. Whether the world as we perceive it really exists, and what its actual character is—we leave the solution of these and other metaphysical problems to the philosophers and the representatives of the various sciences. The place of the individual in the world as he himself sees it, however, and his relationship to the people around him and to the things confronting him each hour of each day—these questions occupy and interest each of us whether we like it or not. The place that each individual must occupy in the struggle for existence is generally determined by his place in society; custom, habit and tradition usually determine the weapons that we use in the struggles forced upon us. Since, in these struggles, the individual scarcely ever stands alone but, actively or passively, in relationship to others, conflicts and compromises arise in our dealings with others. The codification of the courtesy that a person demands or practises belongs to the realm of ethics, and it is our relationship to ethical laws, the laws of the society of which we are part, that interests most people most.

Thus we find that even in the earliest beginnings of philosophy, among the Greeks, it was the ethical problem to which most attention was paid. This, of course, is not a problem that can be solved independently of other philosophical problems, such as logic, metaphysics and especially the theory of cognition, and so we shall have to touch upon these other problems too.

The first scanned page sent by email of the nearly-lost English translation of *Protagoras, Nietsche, Stirner* by Benedict Lachman.

was lost. In May 2018 I was able to track down the translator, not even he had a copy anymore. If Sid kept a copy, it might have been the only copy left.

In the skype call Leon and I talked about a number of things, but I stressed that I thought his father's work was important to save and that I was willing to take it, archive it, put it online for free and publish some of it. I'd already been putting his work online. I shared about my work on DeCasseres, and that I'd contacted John Zube and he was kind enough to sell me some of his microfiche, even though

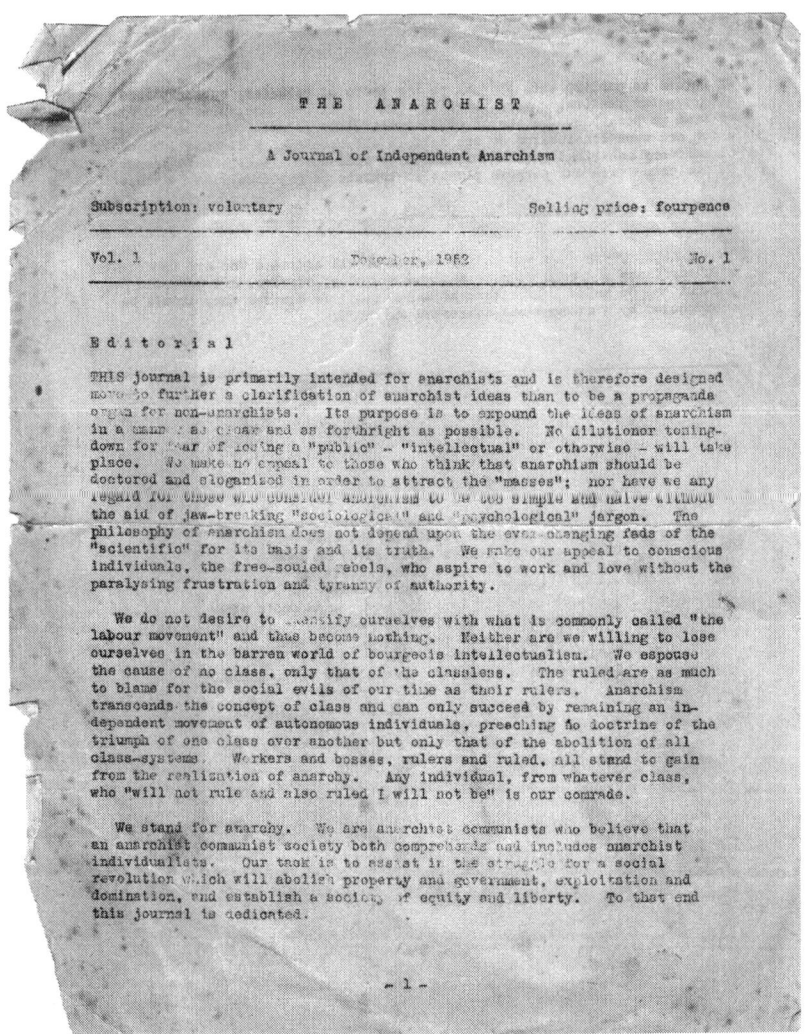

The Anarchists Volume 1, No. 1, December 1952. This is the first journal Sid published.

his Peace Plans project was over for half a decade.[17]

Leon said, basically, if he had to break into the flat while Pat was gone and just take the stuff, he would. Well, I didn't want to encourage that, but if that was the only way to save SEP's literary legacy? I would not protest too loudly.

A few months passed in silence.

$$\notin$$

Some time in late September 2018 I got a message that Leon had just spent the day at Pat's flat and he had 48 hours to clear it out before the council came around to toss anything that was left into the "tip." Pat had been moved to some sort of nursing home. I frantically sent messages to Pól and Jeff. "I'll pay cab fare or gas or if you need to buy boxes and tape or whatever else" I told them, if they could save the archive. I'd mentioned cautiously this to Leon as well, but my feeling was that Leon might begin to see me as a potential source of money... and while I'm not impoverished, I work a "day job" for my rent and meals and then I work freelance graphic design AND have a small publishing company to pay for the Union of Egoists project and other pursuits. I don't have free money but I'm willing to do what is necessary for myself.

Amazingly, Pól and Jeff were able to show up the next day and spent around 8 hours going through the flat looking for anything related to Sid's work. It was a mess. Pat was just hoarding everything and who knows how long it had been like that. I'd requested they take as many photos as they could, photos I saw as they went through stuff and then a bunch after the fact.

In an email to him, after the fact:

Oh, before I forget, if you happen to run across a text titled *Protagoras Nietzsche Stirner* by Benedict Lachmann, translated into English by Dr. Edward Mornin, that would be the only known copy in existence! Sidney reviewed it, but it was never officially published, and I was able to track down Dr. Mornin (who is in his 90s I believe!) and he can no longer find a copy in his own records!

Two days later, I get a response:

---

17   Zube also sold me a few copies of Sid's journals that he had made the microfiche from. www.LibertarianMicrofiche.com

"I've found it looking through piles of papers took out an envelope and it fell out."

∉

At this point Leon became attached to the papers and decided that *he* would go through and archive them. I tried not to be pushy, but stated my case to him plainly and in detail. Leon was difficult to communicate with, and supposedly has dyslexia. His emails show that that may be true.

Leon started scanning materials and sending them to me. The *Protagoras* manuscript was about 100 pages and it took him maybe a month to scan all the pages and send them in batches of 10. He'd mix pages up and he wasn't putting them flat on the scanner at first... it was incredibly frustrating, to be honest. I kept my cool because if I didn't, who knows? He scanned stuff here and there. He insisted he wanted to set up a gallery show before anything was done with the materials. He wanted the British Library to have them, or maybe to sell them to a collector. I hated to tell him that Sid was... kind of forgotten. The people most interested in his legacy were myself and the two guys that spent 8 hours helping him sort through a hoarder house. I wasn't going to fight with him, but I believe that most libraries would probably sit on the material, and *maybe* make it available to scholars, once they were processed through acquisitions. But the British Library, I had the feeling, would have been a safer place than with Leon. Leon is Sid's son, he has the most legal rights to all of it. I was a stranger in another country. I did my best to be sincere and persistent but not too pushy.

∉

In October of 2016 I set up SidParker.com to have a "larger garden" to cultivate Sid's material in. The UnionOfEgoists.com website is meant to focus on 1845-1945, and while SEP is important to the *study* of that period, I wanted to expand into documenting the milieu that developed around his journals, document the current ideas, and not just his study of historical egoism. I wanted a forum where he was center stage. Easy enough to just set up a new website, and the plan was that Leon would send stuff and I'd transcribe it and put it online. I started compiling information and slowly building out the website.

New journals published by Sid were discovered, such as *The Anarchists*, the anarcho-communist newsletter from 1952. There was a

French journal titled *EGO*,[18] edited by Pierre Jouventin, and letters from Jouventin with a plan to merge with Sid's journal and publish a French and an English edition with Sid as the editor. Issue number 9 of Juventin's *EGO* has both S. E. Parker and Benjamin DeCasseres in French. It was exciting to discover these these things but I was always on edge.

I wouldn't hear from Leon for long stretches, and his communications were moody. I was sympathetic, up to a point... I wouldn't ever claim to know how he feels, or what he's gone through, but my goal was preserving the material, and he was getting in the way of that.

I reiterated that I'd like to archive all of Sid's work here in the US. I felt that Leon was too unreliable, and I couldn't shake the feeling that the material just wasn't safe. Leon sent me a terse response implying that if I didn't "back off," well... what would happen wasn't clear. I backed off, and stopped updating the website until the situation clearly changed. Even if I did nothing more to it, it was the best collection of Sid's work online at any point.

2017

At some point in 2017 I got a message from Sid's granddaughter. **Leon was in jail awaiting trial.** It wasn't clear why, and it wasn't any of my business. "Let me know what I can do," I told her, "I'll pay for someone to pack it up and ship the stuff. I'll do what needs to be done."

I felt sympathy for the granddaughter. Not only did she have a shitty grandfather (as it appears he was, in the role of grandfather and father), and grandmother (she has visited Pat, but found her largely uncommunicative), she had a shitty dad.

There was nothing I could do except wait. Every other month I would send her a message... "I'm here, I want to help, let me know what's going on." The updates from her would have different information. He'd be sentenced on *X* date and all his stuff would have to be moved out by *Y* or it gets trashed. That date came and went, things

---

18   There are at least three journals just titled "Ego". The first being by Edward H. Fulton in 1921, the second by Juventin in 1968, and the third by Sid in 1982. One new discovery was *Individualist-Anarchist Publishing and Translation Project Bulletin*. Published just prior to *Minus One*, it actually announced the journal would be named *EGO, which it obviously wasn't.*

were unclear. I'd come to understand Leon was sentenced and began serving his prison time for quite a number of years, but things were still vague.

¢

Many months passed, I was pretty sure all was lost. I'd prepared a booklet titled *The Walford-Parker Exchange*, which has letters published in British philosopher George Walford's journal *Ideological Commentary*. Trevor Blake is Walford's archivist, building and maintaining the exhaustive gwiep.net since 1995. In his introduction to *The Walford-Parker Exchange*, Trevor mentioned how my intentions to give the material a home had been spurned and possibly lost. I put off releasing the booklet in hope that that would, at the end of the day, not be the case. A few months after the date I was told all Leon's stuff would be trashed by, I relented and released the booklet in December.

2018

Another couple months passed and I sent the granddaughter what I thought was for sure a final message on Thursday afternoon, March 22nd of 2018:

> I'm dropping a line, because we haven't chatted in a while. Can you give me an idea if anything has happened relating to the Sid Parker materials? Should I give up? I'm trying not to bother you.

And she responded:

> I'm picking up my dads stuff on Tuesday 27th March. I can't remember if you sent me a list before if anything to look out for.

My jaw must have dropped like a cartoon. After a few seconds of disbelief i gathered my thoughts and responded:

> What if I was to fly out there to help, would that be okay?
> Would I be able to ship Sidney's stuff back home?

¢

The first panic I had was my passport. It had been many years since I renewed it, and I didn't know off hand if it was even valid. I didn't know if I could even leave the country. I was at work and all of a sudden I realized that I had to be in another country in a couple days to pick up an unknown amount of material in an unknown condition from an unknown location. In the middle of looking up flight and hotel information I realized, after about two hours, I could look at my own Facebook page to find photos and the date of my trip to Switzerland. I confirmed it was 8 years ago, and therefore my passport was good.

A dizzying and slightly panicky series of events led from that exchange to getting a flight on Sunday from the Baltimore, Maryland to Iceland and then the UK, getting to my 10x10' hotel room Monday, and from the hotel to the council flat in Peckham, South London at 10am Tuesday morning. What information I was getting from the granddaughter was a bit vague, but she assured me *this was it*. It was fairly uneventful, though a combination of stressful and exciting.

But make it to Peckham by train and foot I did, and a little early. Slowly folks began showing up, waiting for someone with a key or permission and eventually there were about seven other guys there. I was waiting for the arrival of a friend with a car who I'd arranged to take the S.E. Parker materials and ship them for me. Most of the folks were there to extract Leon's extensive record collection and music ephemera to sell on his behalf. "You the one here for Leon's pop's stuff?" I was asked a few times. We made small talk on the sidewalk. Once the guy from the Housing Council showed up, late, we all wedged into the portico ready to get to work. There were about a half-dozen different keys for the front door and I tried every one of them at least five times, increasingly in a systematic, and assertive manner, and *none of them worked*. I felt like I was in a movie, I had a weird sense of detachment. *Someone had changed the lock.* My thoughs were turning dark. Just when I was about to bribe the guy from the housing council to "walk around the corner for a minute," one of Leon's friends piped up: "The last time we were here I left the front window unlocked," and *BAM* I slid past the cramped cadre and was out in the front yard jumping on the ledge from an electric meter and wrenching up the front window to climb in. I found myself in a half-overturned living-room and darted for the front door. It was a pretty standard layout for a rowhouse that had been divided up. A front room, a bedroom, bathroom and kitchen all attached by a single hallway.

I opened the front door from the inside and the rest of the folks piled in and were off to the races. I barely looked at anything, just enough to know if an item was something I needed to take, or not. Nearly all of it was gathered in one spot, and old steamer trunk, but I had to look around because it could be anywhere. I found a few pairs of Sid's glasses in a side-table, and a small pile of items on the other side of the room.

I walked through all the rooms, multiple passes, looking on top of dressers, under chairs. And on my last walk through the hall I stopped to look at what was hanging on the wall, and there i saw Leon had fashioned an event calendar for the process Church of the Final Judgement with a photo of Sid, Pat, the Frenchman Jean-Pierre Schweitzer, and the Australians Bill and Dave Miller. I smiled, shook my head at nearly missing this jem, and pulled it off the wall and outside to the sidewalk where I was staging everything.

The old metal steamer trunk, a few plastic bins and some ephemera in frames was loaded into a hatchback. Since it was licensed park-

Posing in Peckham, holding Sid Parker's personal copies of two books he wrote introductions to: *Might is Right* (Loompanics Unlimited) and *The Ego and Its Own* (London: Rebel Press).

ing only[19] in the spot, I said my quick goodbyes and we drove around the corner to take a few minutes to look through the haul, and take a photo to immortalize the moment. The archives were then spirited away by trusted comrade and were now in safe hands, where they would boxed with care. **I saved the life's work of Sidney E. Parker.**

∉

That next day I spent visiting locals, friends I've had for years but had never met. I had wept openly in front of strangers twice. The first time was with the granddaughter at her house when they had me over for dinner on Tuesday, and then the next day relating the story of the entire journey to Tanya Peixoto who runs bookartbookshop and Alastair Brotchie who runs @tlas Press.[20]

It was less than a week for five large boxes containing extant papers of Sidney E. Parker, including some books, personal effects and two typewriters, to arrive to my house safely, housed in my home office. I've slowly been sorting through the Parker materials and started updating websites within a day. Without having thoroughly gone through it all, I've already discovered so much that has and will continue to inform the work at the UnionOfEgoists.com project, and SidParker.com.

By the time this is published, I will have published the first issue of *The New En Marge* journal, dedicated to the Sidney E. Parker Archives. It will document some of the interesting items revealed in the Archives, and relay the progress of various goals. In a few years, I hope we will be able to issue a book of writings by Sid, with more to come.[21]

---

19   Of course.
20   I left with copies of the @tlas Press Hans Bellmer's *The Doll* book for myself and *A Mammal's Notebook: The writings of Erik Satie* for my wife. Since I was having 5 large boxes of papers, books and journals shipped to my house I uncharacteristically limited myself to only buying these two books on my trip. Any @tlas Press title is worth buying, and I am thrilled that we are featuring an excerpt from the long out of print *Black Letters Unleashed!: 300 Years of Enthused Writing in German* in this issue.
21   *Protagoras, Nietzsche, Stirner* should be available *very* soon.

THREE POEMS
ÉMILE ARMAND (1925)

The Dream

I dream of a country without suffering
where no one groans under the weight of solitude,
and hearts dared to hope,
with no layers of darkness blackening their desires.
A country without tears and sadness,
where happiness would replace torment,
I dream of a country without suffering,
where one could live with integrity.
I dream of a country where all the smells of misery
would be impossible, where neither hunger nor cold
was suffered by anyone, where free, full,
brilliant, life could finally live.
I dreamt of a country where fecund science
would stir in everyone a noble and beautiful desire,
the desire to know, without heavy and burdensome
limits confining the flight of the mind.
I dreamt of a country where without any difference,
without the vulgar goals of gold and honor,
but acting upon the stimulus of common accord
the most diverse projects would be carried out.
It is not in heaven, this country I dreamt of,
It is in our world, full of prejudices and errors,
and from which we would like to flee, towards a new end -
it is upon this bitter world that its foundation awaits.
It is amongst those who are tired of stalling and obstacles,
amongst those who have decided to act here and now
that the radiant sun of all our dreams will shine;
if our will is founded on one alone.

Date uknown, photographer unknown. Care of the Labadie Collection.

Progress or Dementia?

Because, feverish, he says "I can go faster,
And I want to elevate myself higher: As a somber prisoner
I travel the world, which in every way is narrow to me,
To languish in it. I still don't accept
The torrents dotting the skies with their idyll slowly,
And the antique trill of the gallant nightingale,
They are no longer of my time. I would like a push
Towards the new, the unforeseen… or to find in myself
A still-hidden nook. Mountains, oceans, valleys,
Rivers, deserts, forests, lakes, have become
So common. I need to extend into the future,
To know the still virginal tremblings of the infinite blue."
Because he says: "I want to raise myself up as high as the condor
To where the cities flee from my eyes
And where I can no longer see the yellow of the reaped fields
Nor the waving of the grasses in the capricious winds."
Because he invades the domain of the winged ones
And penetrates the skies more every day,
You imagine glorious destinies for man,
And deify his audacious gestures.
You bow, you become delirious, you adore imprudence,
You deck with flowers the altar of the new cult;
Who knows whether it's progress, regression, or dementia?
I prefer to sing to the fertile and fragrant earth.
I don't believe that the rough voice of the motors
Will ever be worth the most timid song of the troubadour,
Nor the peaceful refrain of crystal clear fountains,
Nor the sound of the reaper harvesting the grains.

Sensibility

I'd prefer to tremble in the heat of battle
To hear the crash of cannon's echoing fear
Standing amongst the dead and half dead,
Harvested by the shrapnel,
Than to see your eyes fill with tears.
I'd prefer to face a bandit assaulting me
In the night, in the middle of the woods, see
Shivering rays tear across the sky. But
I cannot resist for a moment
The sad pearls your eyes fashion.
And if others think it is pure laziness,
That I am a child broken by emotion,
I won't respond, it doesn't hurt me.
I have no hatred for those of frozen soul,
But I don't understand those who can see
Their love cry, insensitive and calm.

LAURANCE LABADIE AND HIS CRITICS
HERBERT C. ROSEMAN   (1967)

Laurance Labadie, the last of the individualist anarchists, heir of Warren, Spooner and Tucker has in recent months been dismissed as a veritable fossil by a young Wobbly (who also feels that individualist anarchism is hopelessly bourgeois), characterized by a disciple of Ludwig Von Mises as being "incapable of reasoned thought," denounced as a "cretin" by another young disciple of "Austrian" economics, and attacked for allegedly being "doctrinaire" by a Gandhi disciple.

That these attacks have all been devious on the one hand and namby-pamby and incredibly naive on the other is a measure of the general decay of native American libertarian-radicalism in the last twenty or thirty years. Mr. Labadie is the first to admit that he is a "cantankerous old man" but he would dearly love to see his vilifiers come out with some of that good old "reasoned thought!" It seems it is terribly old-fashioned to declare for a just and equitable program for land and money nowadays. The socialist (& Gandhian) critics of Labadie would like to do away with the awful (money) altogether — the VonMisians and Objectivists want to hold on to all that "time preference" interest. Does our present economic system cause war? Heaven forbid!

That Mr. Labadie's work will survive his critics this writer has no doubt. Tucked away in obscure journals, large reams of stuff virtually unread and unpublished are the making of a mountain of a book demolishing all comers be they socialists, communists, phony free enterprisers and all the other fakirs who claim to speak for "humanity."

For over forty years Labadie has done battle with socialists, communist anarchists, single taxers, equitists, Gesellites, Social Creditors and invariably come out the victor. However be it noted that he has rarely received thanks for his efforts. He has in fact usually been spat upon and dismissed as a killjoy and crank.

Although he envisages a world of economic freedom Laurance Labadie is no system-maker. He believes that real freedom of competition will show soon enough what's what. He is no Utopian either seeing genuine freedom as a goal rather than a place.

Son of Jo Labadie of the famed Labadie Collection, Laurance Labadie has far outdistanced his father as a thinker and polemicist. Laurence Labadie has had the good luck to have been in contact most of his life with all the best that has been written by the libertarian-radical tradition, a tradition that has become extinct as the dodo, a tradition that is now being plagiarized by spokesmen of the status quo who claim to be libertarians — but whose concept of liberty is actually liberty-by-permission which enables them to hold on to their ill-gotten gains.

Labadie is a prophet though no Messiah and the prognosis for prophets in any time or place has not been very good. However if we ever survive this Orwellian world I think the ideas of the "cranks" will bear fruit.

THE ALTRUIST'S CORNER
TREVOR BLAKE   (2018)

"Egoism is the law of the ego" said Malfew Seklew. Egoism is a description of what I do, not a prescription of what I should do or a proscription against what I should not do. Egoism is no more the cause of my ego than Newton's laws of motion are the cause of movement. I am the territory and egoism is the map. Only as it serves me does it matter to me whether anyone is or is not an egoist. One simply does not recruit or exile oneself. Not this One, anyway.

My draw to egoism is the high degree it places on the descriptive over the prescriptive. It has an internal consistency that no other philosophy has. Far more than A = A, I = I. To avoid confusing the territory and the map, it's good to avoid overly promoting egoism as 'something other people should do.' It's also good to keep an eye on critics, who might catch me saluting a flag instead of patting myself on the back.

"The Altruist Corner" is a regular column in *Der Geist*, consisting of a chronological catalog of critics of egoism. The votes are in, and nearly everyone hates the One. Egoism is too far left, too far right, too far outside and too self-centered — or so call the *causists*. Original spellings retained to honor and to shame.

$$\notin$$

Anti-Dühring (Herrn Eugen Dührings Umwälzung der Wissenschaft)
Frederick Engels (Leipzig: Genoffenschafts Buchdruderei, 1878)
Let us assume that Herr Dühring's axiomatics have convinced us and that we are enthusiastic supporters of the entire equality of rights as between the two wills, of "general human sovereignty," of the "sovereignty of the individual" — veritable verbal colossi, compared with whom Stirner's *Ego* together with his *Own* is a mere dwarf, although he also could claim a modest part in them. Well, then, we are now all entirely equal and independent. All? No, not quite all.

$$\notin$$

"Anarchism" (*Glasgow Herald*, February 12 1898, page 4)
From Proudhon the historian of Anarchism is transported across the Rhine to study Max Stirner, Proudhon's contemporary, and the French thinker's German disciple. Stirner is neatly defined as "the German thinker who is carried away by the unchecked flow of his

thoughts far from the path of the actual life into a misty region of 'cloud-cuckoo-land,' where he actually remains as the 'only Individual,' because no one can follow him." Unlike Proudhon, Stirner had never any desire to become an agitator or to reform society in practice. Dr. Zenker's account of Stirner — whose real name, by the way, was Caspar Schmidt — is quite the best that has yet appeared, and perhaps the only one of any length that is accessible in English. Stirner's main doctrine may be described as a ferocious egoism. Right is might. "All existing right is external to the Ego; no one can give me my right, neither God, nor Reason, nor Nature, nor the State;" (had Private Ortheris found a copy of Stirner in the regimental library?) "as to whether I am right or not, there is only one judge and that is myself; others at most can pass a judgement, and decide whether they support my right, and whether it also exists as a right for them. Law is the will of the dominating power in a community. Every State is a despotism, whether the dominant power belongs to one, to many, or to all... " This is a beautifully simple plan for doing away with crime, but we fear that the answer of the natural man will always be that of Alphonse Karr to the proposal for abolishing capital punishment — "*que messieurs les assassins commencent!*"

∉

"Flotsam and Jetsam" (*Buchanan Observer and East Aberdene Adversiter* Number 1890, March 21 1899, page 5)
"The philosophy of power" is the most recent addition our enterprising cousins on the other side of the great herring pond have contributed to the bulky literature of political economy. And is not conducive. It leaves a taste in the mouth, and pain at the heart, for if this philosophy of power be really what the writer conceives to be, then farewell all human sympathy, consideration and regard, and welcome all that is blackest, basset, and most vulpine the worst mortal breast. In this precious "philosophy" might is the only right, and the poor man is merely craven and vanquished fighter, to be kicked for his mean estate, and huddled out of existence when he ceases to be of use to the successful man above him. It is grim doctrine truly, and if became popular I am afraid the author of this philosophy would find himself in a tight corner. It is the philosophy of the pig-trough and the Tammany ring, but if gets proclaimed in this way from the housetops, it were, the power philosophers will probably find that might still lies with mob, and not with the select persons of Wall

Street, and repent them of their rash declaration.

∉

"Flotsam and Jetsam" (*Buchan Observer and East Aberdeenshire Adver-
tiser* Number 1898, May 16 1899, page 5)
Some time ago in this column I alluded to the "Philosophy of Power"
by Ragnar Redbeard, L.L.D., of Chicago. Then I had not fully examined the work in question, and did not wish to say anything definite
until I had read it for myself. I have done so now, and I must say it has
shocked me — even me. Not that I was wholly unacquainted with
the basic truths upon which the work is built. No one who is tolera-
bly well versed in his Darwin can be that. But I was hardly prepared
for the brutal logic which Mr. Redbeard employs to demonstrate the
idea of the survival of the fittest. It is nature red in tooth and claw,
and man without mercy or pity. War, says the author, is the natural
state of man, and it is only slaves, the weaklings and the "good" who
shrink from exercising it. Might is right all over the universe; and
all laws are framed merely to keep the slaves in order. The freeman
and the hero scorn all laws except those which they make themselves.
Says the author:

> I proclaim death to the weakling, and wealth to the strong. I
> request reasons for your Golden Rule and the why and where-
> fore of your Ten Commands. Before none of your printed idols I
> bend acquiescence, and he who saith thou shalt rue is mortal foe.
> Death! I say death to every lie. Gather around me, oh ye death
> defiant, and the earth itself shall be thine to have and to hold.
> What is your 'civilization and progress,' if its only outcome is
> hysteria and downgoing? What is 'government and law,' if their
> ripened harvests are men without sap. What are 'religions and
> literatures' if their grandest productions are hordes of faithful
> slaves? Human rights and wrongs are not determined by justice,
> but by might. I want courage that has made its mind to conquer
> or perish. Courage that asks no quarter even with the knife at its
> throat — unyielding, sullen, pitiless. That is the courage that has
> never turned master's mill. That is the courage that never will
> turn it — that will die rather than turn it.

In this view of the universe there is room for neither mercy nor pity
nor charity. It is a sermon on the text -

Let him take who has the power, And let him keep who can.

It is the creed of the pure individualist who scorns all restraint of an objective kind. There is nothing great but might. Rights are wholly denied, and it is by might that all things are decided. The prizes of earth belong to the strong. The weak are merely rubbish to cleared out of the way. Granted that the animal is all there is in man, this creed would wholly unanswerable, for what applies to lower types applies also to man, and unquestionably on the material plane it is still an eye for an eye and tooth for a tooth. But the fact that man has a soul that abhors cruelty, and is not responsible for the fact that it does abhor cruelty, seems to me to show that man is more than bundle of tissues, brain, and nerves, and that the beyond man in him seeks union with a greater spirit than made wholly manifest in material things. But I do not press this view. I only throw out the suggestion, I know right well that my proofs are poor. The "Philosophy of Power," should be widely read — it is a grand mental tonic.

¢

Anarchy and Anarchists / a History of the Red Terror and the Social Revolution in America and Europe. Communism, Socialism, and Nihilism in Doctrine and in Deed / the Chicago Haymarket Conspiracy, and the Detection and Trial of the Conspirators by Michael J. Schaack (Chicago: F. J. Schulte & Company, 1889)

EUFAULA, April 13, 1886

Dear Comrade Parsons: [...] Anarchism has a very dangerous drift toward individualism, as you may perceive by reading *Liberty*, of Boston, and individualism is bound to generate some kind of a crazy notion and end in despotism. Beware of individualistic Anarchism and stick to the socialistic.

We are in a state of warfare with all the crazes and must use all the weapons of warfare within our reach. Our present weapons — strikes and boycotting — are dangerous, and expulsive if we were to use the ballot. The workers are the many; the masters the few. Before upsetting the government, let us try to use it. Mayors, councilmen, aldermen governors, and so forth, have a good deal to say about how the police and militia shall be used, and judges have a good deal to say when workingmen are prosecuted for claiming their rights. Could not the workers organize to conquer these offices? What do you think of that? What do you think of that?

Salute and Fraternity. FREDERIC TAFFERD

∉

"Table Talk" (*London Daily News* August 19 1902, page 4)

Those who feel themselves sinking under the weight of their own altruism may take comfort from a really remarkable publication entitled *The Eagle and the Serpent: a Journal for Free Spirits and for Spirits Struggling to be Free*. It appears that several of our contemporary's monthly parts have appeared already; but for some reason we cannot guess they have not attracted universal attention. *The Eagle and the Serpent* is devoted to the propagation of envy, malice, and all uncharitableness. [...] This really is, so far as our knowledge extends, a new departure in journalism. No lunatic asylum should be without it. [...] We have alluded to a case of "freak" insurance. Surely our contemporary may be allotted a very high place in the ranks of "freak" journalism.

∉

"Stirner's Ideas in a System of Paranoiac Delusion" by E. Schultze and
  Conolly Norman. *The Journal of Mental Science* Volume L Number
  208 (January 1904) pages 167 — 168.

The author of this paper tells us that the metaphysician, Max Stirner, who flourished in the beginning of the last century, has become popular within the last few years because Reclam has brought him out in a cheap edition, because he suits the Nietzsche fashion of to-day, and because he likewise tones in with anarchism, a cult which has a certain following. The best of these reasons is no doubt the first, yet it might stagger humanity to think what would happen if Reclam began to publish in twopenny volumes the writings of all the minor German metaphysicians, of the mediaeval schoolmen, or of the English divines of the Seventeenth and Eighteenth Centuries. Dr. Schultze has mercifully summarised his very long extracts from Max Stirner, thus:

> Stirner teaches egoism in its extreme form. He is the representative of the utmost individualism. What Stirner can do, that he may do; for him the place of the conception of 'right' is occupied by that of 'might,' and he recognises only rights, not duties. Political laws, ecclesiastical ordinances, moral rules, are for him mere idle phantasms, mere imagination; no authority binds him. What he wishes to-day he can recall to-morrow if it suits him and

seems advantageous. He may encroach upon the rights of others as far and as much as he has the power, and their acts are correct to him as long as they do not interfere with his interests.

Schultze gives a very full history of a female patient who came under his care too late in the case to enable him, indeed, to study the genesis and growth of her delusions, but who presented exquisitely the ideas which Stirner has formulated. Patient's father was epileptic, her mother weak-minded. Patient learned well, but was always odd. Fire-lifting, domestic quarrels, and attempts at suicide preceded the appearance of overt insanity. In her confirmed condition she was a self-contained, retiring, and somewhat depressive person, yet entertained ideas thus expressed:

> If I lie or steal or murder or commit adultery, or strip myself partially or entirely naked, I am yet not consequently a liar, a thief, a murderer, an adulteress, and a vulgar and improper person, but I remain honourable and proper. If, on the other hand, I am compelled to act thus by others and against my will, it is entirely wrong etc. Her standpoint is briefly set out by Schultze in three propositions: (1) what I will is right; (2) I only do what I will, therefore I commit no wrong; (3) what I do against my will, compelled by others, or by necessity or fear, is wrong. Essentially the patient's doctrine is Stirner's with this difference, that Stirner applied the egoism of the logician to all the race, whose state would therefore be that of perpetual and lawless struggle; the patient applied the egoism of the lunatic only to herself — she would be supreme, and all the world her slaves. For Stirner there is neither right nor wrong in the abstract; for the patient right is what she wills, wrong what anybody else wills. She maintains this position with perfect consistency of speech, and with the calm close reasoning of the paranoiac.

Schultze discusses the possibility of his patient having been directly influenced by Stirner — that is, by reading his books or hearing his views — but any influence of this kind appears in the highest degree improbable. He also considers the question of whether Stirner himself was not insane, but concludes that there is not sufficient evidence to form a judgement.

Does not Schultze's patient show a variety of insanity of negation? That this latter condition may be associated with extreme self-esteem is shown in cases of general paralysis; that it maybe partial is also well known; it would be interesting if we found it only in the moral field.

⊄

"Woman as Man's Property / Suffragists and the Present Marriage Contract" by Earl Percy (*Dundee Evening Telegraph*, July 27 1912, page 4)

Suffragists of all shades have welcomed the production of a Socialist weekly paper for women entitled *The Freewoman*, and both they and members of the Church League contribute to it. In order to give an idea of its aims, it may be noted that in the issue of July 11 a letter appears drawing attention to the hardship entailed on women who cannot find husbands, and suggesting nothing less than State-aided establishments where such women can rear children! [*The Freewoman*] is edited by Dora Marsden, B.A. [...]

⊄

"A Shameless Slander" (*Church League for Women's Suffrage*, September 1 1912)

Readers of *The Morning Post* will have noticed with amazement an attack made by Earl Percy upon the Church League for Women's Suffrage in a correspondence which he initiated under the title 'The Suffrage Movement and its Literature.' The correspondence will be found in the issue of July 24th and of subsequent days. Earl Percy originally chose two grounds of attack, to which he subsequently added a third: (1) That the Church League encourages "literature purporting to show the injustice of the generally accepted view of the respective moral standards for men and women"; (2) that the Church League welcomed the publication of *The Freewoman*; (3) that the Church League has acquiesced in militancy. [...] The second charge was peculiarly scandalous. *The Freewoman* is not the organ of any Suffrage Society. After the first few numbers had appeared, it has been ignored or repudiated by every publication which has any title to speak for Suffragists. It has never been mentioned in these pages. It has never been referred to at any public meeting of the Church League. In our private conferences its existence has been deplored. Its doctrines are utterly at variance with all that to us, as members of Christ's Church, must ever remain sacred and inviolable. Yet the charge was made and persisted in, despite emphatic repudiation, on the sole ground that two letters, in which Earl Percy could find nothing to condemn, had appeared in the pages of *The Freewoman* from the pen of one of our members!

¢

"Assertions Before Facts" (*Leeds Mercury*, June 16, 1917 page 4)
Truth telling is one thing, truth thinking another. Max Stirner was of the opinion that truths were as necessary for the brain as potatoes for the body, and both were to be unearthed with equal ease. This is not to assert that the German is Stirneresque, but it is not to deny that the German seems to enjoy a familiarity with the truth that is enjoyed by less transcendental people.

¢

Bourgeois Influences on Anarchism by Luigi Fabbri (circa 1917, translation by Chas Bufe 1987)
Anarchists have always maintained that life is not possible without association and solidarity, and that struggle and revolution are not possible without a pre-existing organization of revolutionaries. But it's more convenient for bourgeois writers to paint us as promoters of anarchy in the sense of confusion, chaos; and they commence to say that we're agents of chaos, enemies of all organization. And with that they disinter Nietzsche and then Stirner. Many anarchists swallow the bait and in seriousness become promoters of chaos, Stirnerites, Nietzscheans, and other similar absurdities. They reject organization, solidarity, and socialism; some even end up sanctifying private property, and in this manner end up playing the game of the bourgeois individualist. Their ideas become, to use the phrase of Filippo Turati, the exaggeration of bourgeois individualism.

¢

"Books and Authors" by Paul Jordan-Smith (*The Los Angeles Times*, August 17 1952)
TIMID LITTLE RUNT. The most egoistic, swashbucking book I ever read (popular around 1910) was called *Might is Right* and the author of that jungle masterpiece called himself Ragnar Redbeard. I imagined him a bloodthirsty giant, but he turned out to be a mouselike, timid little runt, afraid to open his mouth.

FROM THE LIBRARY: *WOMEN AND WAR* BY RAGNAR REDBEARD
KEVIN I. SLAUGHTER   *(1898)*

Women and War is a 5.25"x7.5" saddle-stiched booklet. It came to us in the extant papers and items that constitute the Sidney E. Parker Archives. As seen in photos, the condition would be rated as "poor," with the pink paper cover not only detatched, but missing pieces, covered in non-archival tape, and showing remnants of label adhesive. The first and last leaves of the interior are also detatched.

With all of this, *Women and War* is incredibly rare in any condition. Cornell University Library lists a physical copy in their Kroch Library Rare & Manuscripts department, and the New South Wales State Library in Australia shows a physical copy in their Mitchell Library. All three of these known editions are listed as "Second Edition."

∉

The front cover attributes authorship to RAGNAR REDBEARD, LL, D / (Author of "Might is Right.")

This is followed by three quotes:

"The males fight each other for the possession of the females. —
Charles Darwin

"Of searching eyes, / The sons of men have need, / When fiercely they have to fight.
Oft times pernicious women, / By the wayside sit, / Who swords and valor dreaded."

Lay of Sigdrifa

"The legends tell of a woman fiend, in the charm of her youth so fair, that men would laugh at the warbling cry and rush to die in her lair. It seems to me I have seen her face and felt the kiss of the ghoul, whom nature hath clothed in angel grace and given a vampire soul." —Von Kotze

At the bottom of the cover:

Women and War by Ragnar Redbeard (London: Holbrook & Daniels, 1989) .
Care of Sidney E. Parker Archives, sidparker.com.

Redbeard regularly adapts or alters quotations to suit his own needs, and I was unable to find him using that exact phrase from Darwin, but it appears to be a partial paraphrasing of one of two different quotes. Darwin uses the exact phrase "for the possession of the females" in both *The Variation of Animals and Plants Under Domestication* (London: John Murray, 1869):

> With the males of all gallinaceous birds the use of their weapons and pugnacity is to fight for the possession of the females; so that the tendency in our Game chickens to fight at an extremely early age is not only useless, but is injurious, as they suffer so much from their wounds. The training for battle during an early period may be natural to the wild *Gallus bankiva*; but as man during many generations has gone on selecting the most obstinately pugnacious cocks, it is more probable that their pugnacity has been unnaturally increased, and unnaturally transferred to the young male chickens.

and *On the Origin of Species by Means of Natural Selection, or the Preservation of Favoured Races in the Struggle for Life.* (London: John Murray, 1869).

> *Sexual Selection.*—Inasmuch as peculiarities often appear under domestication in one sex and become hereditarily attached to that sex, the same fact probably occurs under nature, and if so, natural selection will be able to modify one sex in its functional relations to the other sex, or in relation to wholly different habits of life in the two sexes, as is sometimes the case with insects. And this leads me to say a few words on what I call Sexual Selection. This depends, not on a struggle for existence, but on a struggle between the males for possession of the females; the result is not death to the unsuccessful competitor, but few or no offspring. Sexual selection is, therefore, less rigorous than natural selection. Generally, the most vigorous males, those which

are best fitted for their places in nature, will leave most progeny. But in many cases, victory will depend not on general vigour, but on having special weapons, confined to the male sex.

The second quotation on the cover is from the Norse Saga *The Lay of Sigdrifa*, also known as *Sigrdrífumál*. The translation appears to be from *Edda Sæmundar hinns Frða: The Edda of Sæmund the learned: From the Old Norse or Icelandic* edited by Benjamin Thorpe (London: Trübner & Co. 1866).

The actual source of the final quotation is still a mystery, but the author, Stefen von Kotze, was a German writer who visited Australia. Alfred George Stephens in his book *Victor Daley,* quotes Von Kotze as saying "When I write a poem, I lie on a sofa for three days with the pains of a woman in childbed, and when I get up I am as weak as the baby."
Von Kotze died from a stroke in 1909 at the age of 39.

⊄

The inside front cover features an advertisement for *Might is Right*: "Cloth, gilt $1.50, Paper cover 50c, Mailed." to "Adolph Mueller & Co. 108 S. Clark-st., Chicago."
This cloth edition appears to have never been published.

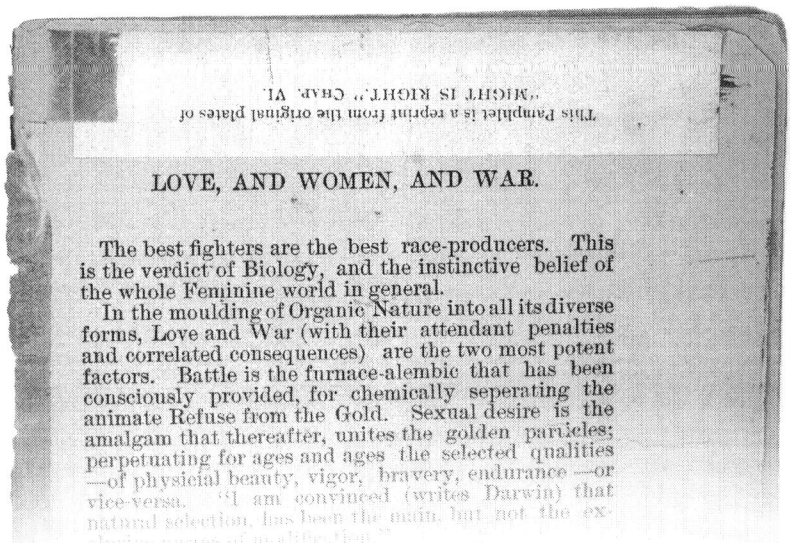

Detail of first page of *Women and War.*

¢

Glued and partially taped to the top of the first page is a piece of paper, with the following legend, upside-down:

This Pamphlet is a reprint from the original plates of "MIGHT IS RIGHT" Chap. VI.

¢

The inside back cover features the poem "Christ: The True Prince of Evil" which is found at the end of Chapter 2 of *Might is Right*. Besides a few typographical errors found here, the poems are the same.

¢

The back cover is full of advertising. The name Adolph Mueller is most likely a pseudonym used for mail order by Arthur Desmond. The entirety of the back cover is reproduced on the opposite page. Thomas Common, one of the first to translate Nietzsche into English, gave *Might is Right* praise in his Nietzschean journal *Notes for Good Europeans*.

We note here the announcement in the middle of the page:

Now being translated MAX STIRNER'S
"THE ALONE MAN AND HIS PREROGATIVES"

The title of Stirner's *Einzige* had been rendered into 8 different variations of an English version before Benjamin R. Tucker declared it to be *The Ego and His Own*. The rendering found here is as unique as many of the others, and found nowhere else. The full story of the translation of the title can be found in my article "An Ego Englished: Anglicizing Der Einzige" in *Der Geist* Issue 1.

The "books by Ragnar Redbeard" section is of interest because it lists an item that, if it existed, appears completely lost: *By Iron and By Blood*. *Blut und Eisen* is the name given to a speech made by Otto von Bismarck given on 30 September 1862, and Redbeard quotes from it in *Might is Right*. Additionally it lists two works "in preperation" that appear to never have been released: *War and Evolution* and *The Roots of Things*.

Adolph Mueller's name and address is listed again as a distributor of the egoist journal *The Eagle and the Serpent*. Ragnar Redbeard constributed writing to that journal.

Back cover of *Women and War* (actual size).

Photo of George Schumm

UNCREDITED   (NO DATE)

George Schumm (1856-1941) was an individualist anarchist and a long-time compatriot of Benjamin R. Tucker. He began publishing German-language publications in his late teens after being in the printing trade for a few years in San Francisco. In 1884 he launched the *Radical Review*, a few years before Tucker published a different journal under the same name. He worked for Tucker for three years in Boston, publishing *Liberty*. He translated John Henry Mackay's *The Anarchists* in 1891. George and his wife Emma Hellar Schumm assisted Steven T. Byington in the 1907 translation of *The Ego and His Own*. Later he worked for the *New York Post* and *The Nation*.

Patrons, a Gratitude
Kevin I. Slaughter & Trevor Blake

Special thanks to our patrons at Patreon. By socializing their self-ishness, they have allowed us to acquire some of the egoist treasures that make up Der Geist and UnionOfEgoists.com. See the address below for details on the rich rewards returned to those who make even the most comfortable of contributions to our cause.

Christine McGuire

Dustin Newman

Eric P. Rowe

Eugene Plawiuk

George Lightfoot

J. S.

Jacob Kirkland

Jim Jesus

JP Quiceno

Logospilgrim

Louis Perrotta III

Luigi Santos-Hammarlund

Matt Godwin

Max Hill

Neil Alvarado

Randi Alan Robinson

Raul Anthony

Reverend Campbell

Richard

Richard Campos

Richard P. Smith

Rob Renstrom

Robert Carmonius

Robert Sherwood

S.

The Independent Ego

Thomas H. Moreland

Waylon Strobehn

WWW.PATREON.COM/UNIONOFEGOISTS

Errata

Der Geist (Volume 1 Number 1 Issue 1) October 2017:
  pg 18, line 15, insert new entry: "The Alone Man and His Prerogatives" / *Women and War* by Ragnar Redbeard / London: Holbrook & Daniels, 1989
  pg 49, line 16, "Southgate" should be "Southport"
  pg 49, line 26, "served" should be "was sentenced to"
  pg 89, line 2 "DeCassers" should be "DeCasseres"
  pg 119, line 6, "opposide" should be "opposite"

The Cynic's Breviary by Nicolas Chamfort (Stand Alone 1065) April 2018:
  pg 2, line 27, "satis- faction" should be "satisfaction"
  pg 3, line 5, "Hence- forth" should be "Henceforth"
  pg 3, line 31, "revolu- tionaries" should be "revolutionaries"
  pg 4, line 16, remove space before "a great ..."
  pg 8, line 21, "dis- trust" should be "distrust"
  pg 11, line 2, "with- out" should be "without"
  pg 11, line 5, "gene- rally" should be "generally"
  pg 15, line 2, remove space after "everything"
  pg 17, line 11, "with- out" should be "without"
  pg 21, line 13, "extra- ordinary" should be "extraordinary"
  pg 24, line 9, remove space after "kings"

The New En Marge (Volume 1 Number 1, Stand Alone SA1083) September 2018:
  pg 2, line 2, "dissnet" should be "dissent"

About the Editors

Kevin I. Slaughter (b. 1975) is a vulgarian and elitist, half son of the South, half child of Mother England. He is a graphic designer and book publisher by vocation and intellectual dissident and misanthropologist by avocation.

He is the Archivist for the Sidney E. Parker Archives (sidparker.com), is the editor for the egoist journal *Stand Alone*, and in 2012 edited *A Bible not Borrowed from the Neighbors: Essays and Aphorisms on Egoism*.

He has lectured at Universities on the topic of Satanism, and an hour long presentation titled "Satanism as Weltanschauung: The Philosophy of the Church of Satan" is available on YouTube.

He admires the outsider genius, the architects of their own worlds - opinions be damned. He is uncomfortable with false dichotomies, understands that however rational he tries to be his consciousness is controlled in part by genetically borne biases and his understanding of the world is skewed by the poor construction of biology that nature has evolved. He's more and more inclined to believe nobody is right, but he's less wrong than most.

Trevor Blake (b. 1966) is the author of *Confessions of a Failed Egoist*, *Max Stirner Bibliography* and *The Eagle and the Serpent Index of Names*. He has written introductions to reprinted books by egoists including *The Gospel of Malfew Seklew* by Malfew Seklew, *For Love and Money* by Leighton Pagan, *The Martyrdom of Percy Whitcomb* by Erwin McCall, and *The Philosophy of Time* by Dora Marsden. Trevor has published 1.2 million words of the British philosopher George Walford at gwiep.net, and *Buckminster Fuller Bibliography* at synchronofile.com. Since 1987 he has published the magazine OVO, details of which are at ovo127.com. He lives in Portland, Oregon.

Made in the USA
San Bernardino, CA
19 November 2018